COURAGE AND BEYOND

10 steps to courageous living

What would you do if
you weren't afraid?

ROSS BUCHANAN & BOB ANDERSON

SRI Publishing
2013

Copyright © 2013 Ross Buchanan & Bob Anderson

All rights reserved. No part of this publication may be reproduced, stored in a retrieval system, or transmitted, in any form or by any means, without prior written permission of the publisher.

SRI Publishing
ross@srigroup.net
www.srigroup.net
www.courageandbeyond.com

Library and Archives Canada Cataloguing in Publication

Buchanan, Ross, 1952-, author
    Courage and beyond : 10 steps to courageous living / Ross Buchanan & Bob Anderson.

ISBN 978-0-9919555-0-3 (pbk.)

    1. Courage. 2. Conduct of life. I. Anderson, Bob, 1962-, author II. Title.

BJ1533.C8B82 2013   158.1   C2013-902692-4

Edited by Jason McRobbie.
Layout and design: Vancouver Desktop Publishing Centre
Special thanks to Denise, Kevin, Colleen and Charleen.

Table of Contents

1. Where to Begin?	7
2. Where Will This Journey Lead?	11
3. What Courage Is . . . And Is Not	13
4. Physical, Psychological, and Moral Courage	15
5. Know Courage: Know Yourself	21
6. The Future, Kid's Today and the Farm League	23
7. From Classrooms to Boardrooms	26
8. Life is a Proactive Sport	28
9. Dream Into Action (and out of fear)	30
10. Be . . . Do . . . Have	32
11. Choice and the Inner Voice	34
12. A Progressive Start to Building Courage	37
13. Our Greatest Fear	40
14. The 10 Steps to Courageous Living	43
The Courage to Be	44
The Courage to Dream	51
The Courage to Trust	59
The Courage to Act	64
The Courage to Listen	70
The Courage to Tolerate	75
The Courage to Reflect	80
The Courage to Speak Up	84
The Courage to Say No	88
The Courage to Adapt	92
15. Personal Action Plan	102
16. Emotional Hijacking	104

17. The Four Fatal Fears	108
Fear of Failure	109
Fear of Being Wrong	110
Fear of Rejection	110
Fear of Discomfort	111
18. Stepping Beyond the Four Fatal Fears	113
19. Courage, Encourage & Discourage	115
20. Responsibility	120
21. Models of Courage	122
Emmie Leung	122
Ted Kuntz	127
Andrew Kemp	133
Dann Konkin	136
22. Conclusion	141

"Courage is rightly esteemed the first of human qualities because it is the quality that guarantees all others."
—Winston Churchill

"Courage is the most important of the virtues, because without courage you can't practice any other virtue consistently. You can practice any virtue erratically, but nothing consistently without courage."
—Maya Angelou

"What would we be capable of if we weren't afraid?"
—The Rest of Us

1
Where to Begin?

If your life is hobbled by the fear of trying and failing, the fear of what others may think, or the fear of what others might say, fear not. What we often forget is our ability to step beyond fear—wherever and whenever we choose.

It takes courage alone.

Instead, we have let fear and its close cousins of anxiety and uncertainty paralyze us in so many ways. The price we have paid is high in terms of not being able to enjoy life to its fullest terms: freedom, joy, health and success.

To face our fears takes courage. Courage becomes fundamental. When fear holds us back, courage needs to set a new gold standard.

Unfortunately, what we face is a courage deficit. In all too many ways, modern life simply does not often call upon us to be courageous. The good news is that these pages hold a solution. The great news is that it works!

As surely as fear is contagious, so too is courage.

Within this book, we offer to step beyond fear, and ultimately, beyond courage. Consider this a field guide for those who wish to strengthen their courage and step into a new dimension of living.

The only real challenge? Consistently choosing courage over fear in all aspects of our lives.

For all the leadership development programs and personal development workshops that organizations send their people to, it's simply impossible to achieve significant and sustainable results without addressing what lies at the heart of all development. Courage. Without courage nothing else really matters does it? It really is what defines us isn't it?

Even with the many modern merits of North American society, we have let the intrinsic fire of courage dwindle. Caution and cowardice have become all too common place in both our workplaces and our lives.

What we specialize in is the creation and cultivation of courage in individuals and organizations to help them achieve their full potential. We have committed ourselves to helping others rekindle that flame and focus their courage to better shape their lives in ways that satisfy them.

The courage deficit that many suffer is very real. It erodes the quality of our lives and dilutes the success of our organizations. This book offers a journey guaranteed to help you strengthen your courage and enhance the quality of your life.

In different ways, following separate paths over the last two decades, we have cumulatively had the opportunity to work with over a thousand organizations and tens of thousands of people. The sum total of our experience revealed a wealth of people who have embraced the true potential of courage in their lives. We honour the unique opportunity with which we have been provided, to witness the courage of so many. Over time, we have been able to get close enough to see what it is that some very special people do to enrich the quality of their lives. True to experience, we found no journey was taken or defined in a single step.

What shone through were the core characteristics that defined their courage. In turn, we recognized the magnitude of opportunity courage offered and considered how to best extend that opportunity. What you hold is the result, but by no means the finished product. Your courage is your own to craft. What we have to share is a path, a plan, call it what you will. For the purpose of these pages, we have called them quite simply:

The Ten Steps to Courage

1. The Courage to Be
2. The Courage to Dream
3. The Courage to Trust
4. The Courage to Act
5. The Courage to Listen
6. The Courage to Tolerate
7. The Courage to Reflect
8. The Courage to Speak Up
9. The Courage to Say No
10. The Courage to Adapt

We will explore each of these steps and show how you can dramatically and immediately alter the quality of your life by changing your learned behaviors in ways that will allow you to become everything that you should, and more importantly can, be in all aspects of your life.

We will focus on The Ten Steps to Courage to enable you to access that which lies deep within us all—and move beyond what holds you back. As upon any journey, some will go further and faster than others. What is important is that you get started and keep going.

2
Where Will This Journey Lead?

We describe that destination as "Courage and Beyond." What lies beyond courage? Think about it. To have courage you must feel fear. Courage is dependent on the existence of fear. To move beyond fear would be a wonderful thing. Freedom awaits, but so does something more.

Think about it as a moving destination and a permanent state of mind offering residency benefits beyond belief. It is a beautiful thing to be in a state of fearlessness of what others might think, say or do—if you do, say or think differently.

What The Ten Steps of Courage offer is the ability to experience a new way of being that results in a freedom wherein joy, love, happiness, bliss and success thrive. Each step makes the question of destination increasingly immaterial. As you take courage to heart, each step makes for a world of difference. Doors open, bridges appear and new ways of being become apparent and abundant.

However dormant, our belief is that courage exists within us all. Our hope is that, as you read this book and complete the exercises, you accept that courage is something you already possess. You may not be using it to its full potential, but without a doubt you have a healthy dose of core courage. This program will help you to access and ignite the full natural benefit of that courage.

There are things getting in the way. Our goal is to determine what is getting in your way and eliminate those factors blocking you from strengthening your courage.

A Courage Self-Assessment
Use a scale from 0 to 10.

How would you rate your current level of courage at home?

0   1   2   3   4   5   6   7   8   9   10

If you were to grow your courage at home in one way what would it look like?

_____

_____

If you were able to achieve this what would the results look like?

_____

_____

How would you rate the current level of courage at work?

0   1   2   3   4   5   6   7   8   9   10

If you were to grow your courage at work in one way what would it look like?

_____

_____

If you were able to achieve this what would the results look like?

_____

_____

3
What Courage Is . . . And Is Not

We are by no means the first to try and explain courage. However, there is no clearly defined test for courage. One of the problems with defining courage is that it is considered to be implicit. We expect people to know what we mean when we use the word. As a result, the word "courage" has acquired a sweeping range of meanings.

In reality, courage has been used to describe everything from the most banal to the most extraordinary actions. For example, young people in general are predisposed to engage in high-risk activities. Knowing this, would riding a motorcycle at a high rate of speed through heavy traffic to get to work on time be courageous or reckless? To the majority of rational adults, this would be perceived as reckless. To the teenager on the bike, and his friends, this might be deemed courageous. Depending on who you are and where you are in life's cycle, courage is subjective.

Most often, courage is associated with acts of virtue and heroism. However, even here the lens of perception holds court. For example, the pilots who flew jet airliners into the Twin Towers in New York City on September 11, 2001 carefully planned their mission down to the last detail. They executed their plan knowing full well what the result would be, and they believed with every fiber of their being that they were doing the right thing. Was it a courageous act? Were the Japanese Kamikaze pilots of the Second World War courageous? Was dropping the bomb on Hiroshima and Nagasaki courageous?

Tough questions with no easy answers. Perhaps it takes more courage not to go to war.

That said, the "damn the torpedoes" kind of courage rarely floats for long. Without question, the intellect plays a key role in defining courage. What we encourage is the kind of courage that flows from clear thought and rational thinking. This most often results in solutions that reduce the risk and achieve the desired results without undue damage.

It is important to note that bravery is not courage. Bravery and courage are often confused because they are closely aligned, but they differ. A recent study for the *International Journal of Leadership* conducted by David H. Hartley of Clarion University noted:

> "Bravery (is) an immediate response to an imminent threat to the individual, and may be a reflexive response by someone who in other circumstances would not be considered to possess courage. Courage, on the other hand, (is) a long-term character quality that serves as a foundation for brave acts."

Courage, we offer, is the cornerstone for healthy human development. As such, while it serves as the foundation for bravery and the font of all heroic acts, its definition is not so neatly delimited.

4
Physical, Psychological, and Moral Courage

There are three basic types of courage: physical, psychological, and moral.

Facing physical threats is one thing most of us are rarely required to do, thanks largely to those who remove these threats as part of their jobs. These people are those for whom courage is a job requirement: the armed forces, the fire department and search & rescue services to name a few.

On the other hand, the psychological and moral courage required to deal with daily life in a healthy manner is something that benefits us all to explore further.

Physical courage is relatively self-explanatory. It's the courage employed in protecting your physical self or that of another. Moral and psychological courage are a bit more mysterious for two basic reasons. They happen in your head and are therefore not always immediately obvious to others. They also lie closest to the heart of courage.

Moral courage is what it takes to be true to yourself and your sense of right and wrong. Psychological courage is what's required to maintain sanity and control your emotions—to be applied appropriately in a healthy way. Neither is easy—we all face moral and psychological dilemmas daily.

A BRIEF EXERCISE

Earlier we identified the three basic kinds of courage as physical, moral and psychological. Take a moment now and rate yourself on all three types of courage:

Write down a recent example of when you were "Physically Courageous."

_____

_____

On a scale from 0 to 10, rate your sense of "Physical Courage." Then, on the same scale, mark where you want to be.

0   1   2   3   4   5   6   7   8   9   10

Write down a recent example of when you had to use "Moral Courage."

_____

_____

On a scale from 0 to 10, rate your sense of "Moral Courage." Then, on the same scale, mark where you want to be.

0   1   2   3   4   5   6   7   8   9   10

Write down a recent example of when you had to use "Psychological Courage."

_____

_____

On a scale from 0 to 10, rate your sense of "Psychological Courage." Then, on the same scale, mark where you want to be.

0   1   2   3   4   5   6   7   8   9   10

The gaps between where you are and where you want to be are what we will bridge.

Conditioning Our Courage

Do you need fear to be courageous on a daily basis? Earlier we said that in order to be courageous you must first feel fear. True enough—at first. Faced with danger or risk, fear is a natural response. However, as shown the world over, fear can be transformed into focus by individuals and teams trained to step beyond courage in the course of daily duty.

Consider this story of courage: The local Search and Rescue team is called out to rescue three fishermen whose vessel is sinking in a storm off the coast. The team responds immediately; they file into the helicopter and take off into steadily worsening weather. Targeting the mayday signal, they arrive; the pilot hovers over the sinking boat while one man operates the winch that lowers another down to the boat. The helicopter is battered with wind; the man on the line, though soaked and thrown about, lands on the deck of the sinking boat amidst the storm. Decisions are made in an instant as time is limited. He attaches the first sailor to himself and the winch. With a signal he ascends. The two remaining men know he will return, and on this day, all live to share the tale.

While this story is full of courageous acts, there is no fear on the rescuers' behalf. This is a result of training and preparation for such events. In the case of Search and Rescue teams, they train intensely in the field under constantly changing conditions against varying real-life scenarios. By the time that training goes into practice, they have reached a state of fearlessness. Repetition and routine have enabled them to overcome the fear that called forth their courage the first day on the job. Does this make their work any less courageous? Hardly. Instead, it points to something more.

Research Psychologists Woodward and Pury in 2007 altered their definition of courage by removing the concept of fear as a necessary lens through which to interpret courage:

> "Courage is the voluntary willingness to act, with or without varying levels of fear, in response to a threat to achieve an important, perhaps moral, outcome or goal."

Regardless of the deserved respect it regards for those so trained or inclined, fear remains most relevant to the discussion for most of us. Why? For starters, we're wired that way.

Courage, Fear and Snakes on a Brain

A pair of scientists, Uri Nili and Yadin Dudai from the Weizmann Institute of Science in Rehovot, Israel, wanted to see if they could map the brain function of courage in the face of fear. They did something very interesting—using a snake.

They equipped a MRI machine with a conveyer belt near the subject's head. On the conveyer belt they affixed a live snake that the subject could both see and control through a mirror. The individual being mapped was in full control of moving the snake 'closer' or 'further away' via a hand held device.

Nili and Dudai's study considered three primary means of measurement. They measured brain activity with the MRI scanner and sweat rates with electrodes; after all, fear and sweat go hand in hand, right? Simultaneously, the subjects filled out a questionnaire regarding how fearful and/or anxious they felt throughout.

When the questionnaires and electronic findings were analyzed, an interesting finding emerged. There are fearless sweaters. There are those who fear but do not sweat.

That's not the really interesting part though. Wherever this paradox existed in the participant's reactions, he or she would act courageously and continually move the snake closer. Only those whose physical and questionnaire responses exhibited both sweat and fear moved the snake away. For them the fear was very real, regardless of the absolute control on hand and safety of the setting.

Where is the driver in the brain for all of this? During the test, Nili and Dudai monitored brain activity in the volunteers and noted something of interest in the subgenual anterior cingulate cortex (sgACC). Bringing the snake closer to the head strongly activated the sgACC. This was the only region of the brain to show activity each time the subject moved snake closer in the mirror. The more the participants were afraid, but did not succumb to their fear, the more active the sgACC became, as if more "mental effort" was required to act in the face of fear.

For those that did succumb to the fear, another region came into play: the amygdala, an area known as the seat of primitive fear, among other things. Interestingly, just as courage is required to overcome fear, only a strong activated sgACC silenced the amygdala responses in this experiment.

At least on a screen, the mechanics of courage in the brain appears to involve a competition between the amygdala and the sgACC. When fear reaches a certain threshold, without the sgACC interfering and suppressing the bodily fear, the test case succumbs to fear. The amygdala may be the brain's fear centre, but internally the sgACC is our own internal Search and Rescue, serving to control and suppress bodily fear responses and send nerve projections into the amygdala to shut it down as needed.

Why should we care about this? Of course there is a "brain correlate" to whatever we say, think, or do. So what? Simply put, if your amygdala continually overpowers your subgenual anterior cingulate cortex you will be perpetually petrified. While you need not become a neuro-scientist, brushing up on basic brain science is reassuring. In a world that can appear hard-wired for fear, knowing that our brain is similarly hard-wired for courage is inspiring. Putting that knowledge to use in our own lives is priceless.

5
Know Courage: Know Yourself

Back to the question of what defines courage for a moment. It's a state of mind, a level of consciousness and surety of self which belongs to us all. It precedes the brave and defines those whose duty summons it daily. It is the ember that ignites the rocket fuel that compels you to take action.

It is the force within that liberates you from fear's most debilitating impacts.

So why do some people seem to have an abundance of courage, and others so little?

An abundance of courage comes from knowing clearly who you are and that for which you stand. It is a result of clarity, knowing what right and wrong mean in your own mind, words and actions. It comes from being aware of what your personal limits or tolerances are for those things that conflict with your personal and/or shared values.

A BRIEF EXERCISE

Let's test this a little. Does it make sense to say that your level of courage is related to the amount of value you have for life? How far would you go to protect your own life? How far would you go to protect the lives of others you value such as your children, your immediate family, your spouse? What about your property? To what extent would you be courageous in protecting your property? True enough, fairly common questions.

What about being truthful? When was the last time you did not tell the truth? Most of us won't have to think back too far. In fact, we would not be able to function in society today if we told the truth all the time.

It's no lie that it takes courage to tell the truth, especially when we are fearful of what might result. In such cases, not telling the truth is easy to justify. *"It might get me and someone I care about into trouble." "I don't want to hurt their feelings." "They will think less of me if they knew the truth."*

The truth is, with enough courage, we can all handle the truth.

The real question is how much do you value the truth? Or better yet, where do you draw the line when it comes to telling the truth?

Would you lie to yourself? No? Good. Then accept that you have nothing to fear from the truth of what drives you. It took courage to pick up this book. You are looking to apply a courage you already possess. True courage carries a deep sense of self, of knowing who you are and what you stand for. This marks an excellent beginning for any journey—and perfect timing for the present moment.

6
The Future, Kid's Today and the Farm League

As discussed, we believe there is a courage deficit at present and the future of courage looks even worse. If you think we have a courage deficit today in North American society, consider the legacy of such an intrinsic lack—in our boardrooms and playgrounds alike. Fortunately, no one can change that future as readily as you. In general, what we really lack are appropriate models of courage.

Past generations suffered true crises as part of daily life and courage was quite simply that which was required. The halls of history are lined with courageous acts. Where did that courage come from? Likely necessity.

More importantly, where has it gone?

We have a personal theory that the further we drifted from our agrarian roots, the more 'civilized' we became. Over a few short generations in North America, we abandoned rural life to arrive where we are today: civilized, citified and living a cautionary tale. We lost the opportunity to develop courage as intended—in the natural course of childhood development with the challenges of nature on our doorstep.

Consider the case of the typical North American youngster—they are protected, raised in an urban environment, too often sheltered from the opportunity to wander, explore, risk and learn. That shelter becomes a shell for many and a hell for some. As adults, many find it difficult to respond to situations that demand what they lack most, and is most simply, courage.

Deprived of role models and opportunities to explore courage in their early development, cowardice and caution become constant companions for young and old alike.

We know that courage is not present at birth. There is not a courage gene. Courage is developed and nurtured through learning, experience and exposure to risk. However, many children are no longer afforded the opportunity to summon courage in the face of life's myriad challenges.

We think kids from the country still hold an edge today. Without a doubt, children raised in rural areas have a greater opportunity to cultivate their courage and, as a result, they are often more successful in life. Though they might gravitate to the urban environment in time, their farm-grown courage carries over into all aspects of their life.

Courage grows naturally in the great outdoors. With the freedom to explore nature and life with all of its opportunities and responsibilities, the world at their doorstep is an incredible gift to which urban children simply do not have ready access—if any. Consider that in the country the average 12 year old can explore nature in their backyard, drive a truck, ride a horse and run a tractor.

Compare that to the life of the average city kid these days. The average 12 year old in an urban environment can do none of the above. In many well-intentioned ways they are cheated of the opportunity to grow their courage and confront fear—at least beyond the classroom and game console. Sitting in a room playing computer games, however, is not the environment in which courage is encouraged.

The culture of fear that pervades so many urban settings results in children being raised in a protective bubble. What we see often later in life are young adults with an immature moral compass who are psychologically unprepared—addicted to caution, comfort and convenience. Beyond that, they deeply fear anything that pushes them outside of the protective bunker that has carried them from the cradle.

What we write on the minds of our children is to be safe. We ourselves are cautious for fear of exposing them to danger. For better or worse, we all know that life is full of risks.

The solution? Wherever and whenever, we encourage parents to get their children out into the country or the wilderness to explore. Whatever gifts we give our children, there is no substitute for courage; it is the base upon which all else is built, appreciated and dreamt. In our experience there is no finer courage incubator in existence than exposure to a rural way of life or some time in the wilderness.

We understand the concerns that urban parents have for their children. The city can be a very dangerous place. For the first time in the history of civilization though, the wilderness actually holds fewer dangers than the city.

Let's be clear. We are not recommending that you drop the kids off at the edge of the forest on a Friday night and tell them that you will pick them up on Monday morning before school. What we are saying is that if you are a parent or guardian of a young person, take the time to get outside. Share the experience with them and give them the opportunity to learn. The country just happens to be a great place to do this.

7
From Classrooms to Boardrooms

Given the fact that many young people are losing the opportunity to cultivate courage early in life, are we surprised to find an absence of courage in business later in life?

Corporate culture most commonly does not encourage courage. Cowardice and caution are more common crutches with their own support systems. Is it really any wonder that so many businesses continue to crumble on so many fronts?

Caution is about playing defense. If we are always playing defense we will never win. We need courage at all levels of business and given the urgency of the crisis we need it now. We are in desperate straits at a critical turning point. Can we turn it around? Maybe. With a bit of courage.

Courage is what it is all about. It is the missing piece of the puzzle at work and at home. As is known, you cannot fix what you do not acknowledge. If we admit to gaps in our own courage and step up to make a concentrated effort to grow that courage, we stand to fix many things. For starters, we are going to enhance the quality of our lives and pass on these skills to our children.

You can also turn around a struggling or mediocre performing organization. By instilling courage at the heart of an organization, by showing other people how to strengthen their courage, and by rewarding and modeling courage you can turn any organization around in under a month. Yes . . . 30 days.

It's not just the organization, but the lives that give it breath. The presence of courage in all areas and at all levels of an organization instantly and immediately transforms the culture—and courage-filled cultures produce exciting new results.

The sad reality for at least nine out of 10 organizations is a corporate culture of fear. That said, corporate culture stems from corporeal reality; for a corporate culture to be one of fear then it follows that many of the people who populate the organization are either plagued with fear—or have given up.

8
Life is a Proactive Sport

> "To keep our faces toward change and behave like free spirits in the presence of fate is strength undefeatable."
>
> —Helen Keller

The topic of courage is not something that many people talk about these days. When we do hear discussions of courage it is centered on society's protectors: police, firefighters or soldiers. Where would we be without people who took the risks?

Without realizing what has happened in the last decade or so, many of us have overemphasized personal safety and caution in our lives. As a result we are now living our lives on defense rather than offense. Think of Stephen Covey's wonderful book *The Seven Habits of Highly Effective People* where he builds a powerful case for living life proactively rather than reactively.

Albeit often comfortably enough, life becomes mired by reactivity. Rather than dreaming big, we play it safe and await what comes. When we choose to play "not to lose" in the great game of life, there is little excitement or reward to be gained. If instead, we play to our fullest, the great game grows its offering.

How many people do you know who cling to a less than satisfying life rather than dreaming and doing exactly what their heart tells them they should be doing? Are you one of them?

It is easy to allow the fear and caution engrained in our minds to drown out the truth that is screaming from our hearts and souls. Who writes your brain's soundtrack? Some of the tracks that get stuck in our heads . . . *be careful, don't rock the boat, play it safe, it is good enough the way it is, you can't do better, nobody will listen* . . . keep us stuck in a life diluted by anxiety, discomfort or fear.

While such self-oppressive thinking limits one's proactivity, it is as common as the cubicle and the shuffle of the "walking, talking dead" that populate our streets, homes and work.

Encased in safety, why does it seem our fears have become magnified? Sure there are real dangers in life that need to be avoided, but why do so many people spend each waking moment drowning in a sea of artificial fear?

Risk might well be everywhere, but the real dangers are few and far between for the majority. It is as if we are living our entire lives on Code Orange, escalating concerns, worries and anxieties to full-fledged Fear.

Unfortunately, there are those for whom it works very well to have the mass population in this state. They are the fear mongers. They are bullies. They are among us. Take courage; they are weak.

In our coaching capacities people tell us about what makes them uncomfortable: in general and in detail. We have our own challenges, but do we let it paralyze us? No. We act in the face of our fears. The action may be as simple as speaking the truth about an issue or letting someone know how we feel about their behavior, but these are the simple things that hold so many of us back. It is about being committed to doing what we know we have to do to get what we want in life . . . even if it is a little uncomfortable.

9

Dream Into Action (and out of fear)

> "Life shrinks or expands in proportion to one's courage."
>
> —Anais Nin

Why are so many people afraid to imagine what their lives might look like if they had the courage to dream? Even those who are bold enough to dream seldom move to the next step of creating an Action Plan and executing those actions. Why? It's likely due to fear of failure or what others might think, say or do.

We have been groomed to fear-based thinking. Unfortunately, we are in fact giving our power away to it. We are also making it something other than what it most often really is: anxiety, discomfort, concern, or worry.

The sooner we accept that 99.9 percent of what we call fear is so much less—the better for everyone except the fear monger. Think of the possibilities that exist in your life if you stare down those imaginary fears and reclaim the far more powerful life that you have been denied.

For many of us the list of potential fears is extensive. Some examples that we often hear include the fear of: failure, rejection, going broke, being alone, humiliation, public speaking, being ostracized by family and friends, physical discomfort, regret, success, trying, conflict and trust.

What holds *you* back? If our fears are the anchors that keep us stuck, what keeps you from moving forward and embracing joy and happiness in your life? If you were free of your fears how would you live your life? What would it look like? What would you do if you weren't afraid?

What if you even learned to enjoy the things you currently fear? Would you speak up more often, talk to more strangers, ask more questions and dive headlong into those projects you've been dreaming about? What kind of difference would that make in your life?

What we often hear from one of the sexes, and it isn't women, is that they aren't afraid of anything. These bullish brethren have built too many defenses and bring us the most reward when they bring down their walls. They offer ample justification for why they don't speak up, or talk with strangers, or ask a question, or jump into a project—and of course, it has nothing to do with being afraid. Over the years, we have heard it all too many times to count: *they really didn't have anything to say . . . they didn't want to be rude . . . they didn't think the time was right.*

The truth is that when you are able to move beyond these rationalizations and the crazy stories we tell ourselves and hide within—everything changes.

How good could it be? What sort of success might you enjoy?

10
Be . . . Do . . . Have

> "Courage is not the absence of fear, but rather the judgment that something else is more important than fear."
>
> —Ambrose Redmoon

> "Courage is being scared to death, but saddling up anyway."
>
> —John Wayne

Ross couldn't resist the John Wayne quote. Just the other day someone handed him a card and on it was the Code of the West. He found the very first of its ten principles particularly affirming: 'Live each day with courage.'

'It isn't just for cowboys anymore,' the man in the hat told Ross. Not surprisingly, he agreed in full. We committed to working on this book shortly thereafter.

Years ago Ross was fortunate to participate in a personal development program called *Choices* which was led by Thelma Box. Years later, one of its key messages rings as true as ever. *Be committed to do what you have to do to get what you want. Be . . . Do . . . Have.* These three words speak to the heart of courage, but the bare truth is found in the middle. Quite simply, we need to do. In the face of fear, we need to take action.

Do you think that people who act with courage regularly don't feel fear? Of course they do. What they do differently is move past the fear; they don't let it paralyze them or lead them astray.

Alternatively, people who lack courage will feed their fear almost reflexively; this the long-term effect of strengthening the fear. Yes, we are actually feeding the fear in our lives. When you avoid facing a fear, you then feel relieved that you escaped it. This psychological feedback rewards the avoidance behavior, making you even more likely to avoid facing the fear in the future—and negating the opportunity for greater reward.

Does this apply to you? Has avoiding asking someone for a raise, an order or out on a date ever led to happiness? Why then are such things so common?

We are literally conditioning ourselves to become less courageous and more timid. The truth for many is that we have built our way of being upon a foundation of fear and that makes change very difficult. While is not impossible, and is indeed the reason we are writing this book, the longer the fear has been nurtured, the more difficult the escape may prove.

Fear has become our drug of choice. As surely as we are consumers of fear, so too are we addicted to their avoidance. In gated communities, fear has become a status symbol. We get a rush or a reward when we "avoid" our fears. What we do not achieve is a full life.

Our experience is that while nobody really wants to live a life polluted by fear, few know how to live without it, let alone how to free themselves. In this Field Guide we will show you exactly "how" to escape the toxic poison of fear.

11
Choice and the Inner Voice

"Most of our obstacles would melt away if, instead of cowering before them, we should make up our minds to walk boldly through them."

—Orison Swett Marden

Fortunately, our experience is that escaping fear is always possible. After all, our ability to access our courage never leaves us. It is always there. At present, it might be the smallest flame, but courage remains. It never goes away and offers a constant reminder of what your life could and should look like.

Then there is that little voice—it reminds us that we should drop 20 pounds, move to an organization that appreciates us more, be in a much more loving relationship and that we are meant for bigger and better things. More importantly, we could. We can.

The truth is that this inner voice will never stop until the day we die, constantly chirping away at us. At times louder than others, but always there, it reminds us of what could have been. As with the amygdala, to quiet the voice, you need only refocus.

Want to silence the inner voice that is chewing away at your self-esteem and confidence?

The solution is both immediate and significant. Figure out what you want and decide what you have to do to achieve what you want. Take the action required to achieve what you want to do with your life.

Sure, it takes courage to achieve that for which our authentic self searches—but what is the alternative?

Unfortunately, the alternative is all too common. Typically, we silence the voice: drowning it out with work and distraction, sedating it with alcohol or drugs. When we consider what has to be done, we feel overwhelmed by the apparent magnitude of the task. We rationalize not taking action: *we are not capable, we are not allowed, we don't deserve the rewards.* It becomes easier if we just leave things as they are.

The voice may be temporarily silenced, but are we happy? No. To block out that inner voice is to simply grow numb to the reality of our authentic selves.

The reality is that if you break down what has to be done to achieve any goal, the steps become clear and potential becomes possibility. There is only one thing immediately easier—not doing it. We already know what we might do differently. We know that we are cheating ourselves of a full and joyous life. Therefore, we also know what we need to do to get back on track—or at least our inner voice does.

A BRIEF EXERCISE

So what is your inner voice asking you to do? What is it telling you to do?

Leave. Quit. Stay. Commit. Speak. Write. Dance. Act. Exercise. Ask. Love. Switch. Move on. Let go. Learn. Forgive.

Whatever you get from this, write it down. What does your inner voice tell you that you need to do about your life? This is the starting point on an exciting journey, one that will reward you, however you choose to define it, with success in life. The good news is that courage does not need to change your world upside down completely and immediately. We can be gentle with ourselves and cultivate our courage.

_____

_____

That said, first we need to walk through the fear. Are you ready to step past the stories you tell yourself that keep you from taking action? Are you seriously committed to taking the past out of your future and growing your courage?

Good. Then, let us suggest a great way to start.

12
A Progressive Start to Building Courage

This approach is similar to progressive weight training. Training yourself to lift 200 pounds isn't so hard if you train to do repetitions with 150 pounds. We begin with a good weight, something challenging, but ultimately—doable. Something you can feel good about lifting. With focused conditioning, the heavier weight is then lifted with ease.

Similarly, speaking in front of an audience of 200 people is far easier once you have addressed a crowd of 20. This approach to the incremental growth of your courage is designed to help you achieve what most people seldom do—get out of the gate and into the world of greater opportunity.

A QUICK EXERCISE

Whatever you fear most, write down the three things you could do to get out of the gate and get started.

1. _____

2. _____

3. _____

Congratulations! That took courage. 'Only in your head,' or 'only in a few simple words', you might say. We say that is psychological courage at its finest.

In order to write these things down, you had to confront fear and take action. You have just used your courage to take the first step. Well done—let's revisit your list.

Which of your three action items is most easily accomplished? Which poses the biggest stretch? Which would generate the least anxiety? Start there and you are bound to impress yourselves with the results.

Following this simple process, you accomplish two things. You cease reinforcing the fear/avoidance response that you exhibited in the past and condition yourself to act more courageously moving forward. Living up to even the smallest action item on your list is a major accomplishment. Remember, fear is diminished in the face of courageous acts of all sizes.

Let us share a funny truth before we embark most fully on The 10 Steps to Courageous Living. After all, you have a right to know. We have our own fears, one in particular that may surprise you. Though we do it regularly, neither of us feel totally comfortable speaking to large audiences.

Our personal comfort zone is facilitating small group conversations where there is an exchange of ideas. Speaking to a large audience is more often talking at, rather than speaking with, a group of people. What have we done to move beyond this fear? We make a point of accepting every invitation we receive to speak with larger audiences.

An action plan only counts once put into action. When it comes to growing your courage, intention isn't good enough. Your intention needs attention. The best way to create that attention is by following this plan to get started on the growth you seek. What really matters is that you do it.

Just as muscles atrophy if they are not regularly stretched, your courage will atrophy if you do not consistently challenge yourself to face your fears. In the absence of conscious conditioning, we become weak in body and mind alike. Fear gains strength by default until it defines and delimits our lives. Until we draw upon our courage, there is no middle ground.

Keep that in mind throughout this book and your greater journey. We need to embrace our greatest fears—those within—for what they are: the opportunity for growth throughout all aspects of our life.

13
Our Greatest Fear

> 'The highest courage is to dare to appear to be what one is."
>
> —John Lancaster Spalding

If we might all agree that Spalding's words are ones to live by, why do so few of us seem to know who we really are, let alone dream of what we might accomplish? That is why we begin the first of The 10 Steps of Courage with 'The Courage to Be You.'

Courage is something you can only truly cultivate alone. It is a private victory, not a public one. Summoning the courage to listen to your innermost desires is *not* a group activity and does *not* result from building a consensus with others.

Kahlil Gibran writes in *The Prophet*, "The vision of one man lends not its wings to another man." Without a doubt the purpose of your existence is yours alone to discover. Whether you live alone or enjoy the deepest intimacy of a loving partner, deep down you must still face the reality that your life is yours alone to live.

What you do with your life isn't up to your parents, your boss or your spouse. It's up to you and you alone. You can choose to temporarily yield control of your life to others: whether it is to a person, a company or simply to the pressures of daily living. What you can never give away is your personal responsibility for the results.

Whether you choose to proactively create your own life or merely react to life—you and you alone must decide.

As you commit to following the path offered by The Ten Steps of Courage, you will ultimately confront what is perhaps the greatest fear of all—that you are more powerful and capable than you realized, that your true potential is far greater than anything you've imagined, and that with this power comes tremendous responsibility.

You may not be able to solve all the woes of this planet, but if you commit yourself to the fulfillment of your true potential, you will make a significant impact on the lives of many. You can count on that playing forward for future generations.

Author Marianne Williamson captures our potential well with her words:

> "Our deepest fear is not that we are inadequate. Our deepest fear is that we are powerful beyond measure. It is our light, not our darkness that most frightens us. We ask ourselves, Who are you to be brilliant, gorgeous, talented, fabulous? Actually, who are you not to be? You are a child of God. Your playing small does not serve the world. There is nothing enlightened about shrinking so that other people won't feel insecure around you. We are all meant to shine, as children do. We were born to make manifest the glory of God that is within us. It's not just in some of us; it's in everyone. And as we let our own light shine, we unconsciously give other people permission to do the same. As we are liberated from our own fear, our presence automatically liberates others."

Ask yourself this. What is the difference between you and one of the truly courageous, legendary figures who had a huge impact on others? You and Gandhi were both born with talents and weaknesses. You and Martin Luther King shared many of the same fears. What makes them any different is that they did not submit to their weaknesses and fears. Moreover, they were fearless in their determination to see the world change for the better. They saw the greatness of spirit within us all.

Catching a glimpse of your own greatness can be one of the most unsettling experiences imaginable. That is why Williamson calls it "our greatest fear." Even more disturbing is the awareness of the tremendous challenges that await you if you accept it.

Following the path to courage is not easy and it requires making the committed decision to permanently let go of the meekness and weakness within you. The first few times you face down your fears, you may quickly retreat back to the illusory security of life and the dual addictions of comfort and convenience. If you keep exercising your courage, you will eventually grow to the point where you can openly accept the challenges and responsibilities of life as a fully conscious human being. Continuing to live in fear will simply hold no more interest for you.

You will no longer be content as a member of the walking, talking dead. Take action! Without a doubt life rewards such action, and as you may have experienced, penalizes inaction.

As in sports, penalties can be expected when there are no goals.

14
The 10 Steps to Courageous Living

Earlier we introduced you to the 10 Steps to Courageous Living. We are now prepared to take that first step to strengthening your core courage. First, let's revisit the core set of courage muscles we will develop:

1. The Courage to Be

2. The Courage to Dream

3. The Courage to Trust

4. The Courage to Act

5. The Courage to Listen

6. The Courage to be Tolerant

7. The Courage to Reflect

8. The Courage to Speak Up

9. The Courage to Say No

10. The Courage to Adapt

We will now explore each in turn and reveal how you can dramatically alter the quality of your life.

The Courage to Be

> "This above all, to thy own self be true."
> —Shakespeare

Our personal experience is that true freedom in life is only possible when you free yourself from needing the approval of others. We have come to the realization that there are people who are "internally validated" and people who are "externally validated."

Internal validation is the key.

People who are externally validated need the constant approval of others. It is all too common in today's society. The addiction to external validation turns people into puppets who dance to someone else's music. Do you see how quickly that takes us from our authentic self?

People who are internally validated are free to express themselves fully, openly, and genuinely. They are authentic. They are real. So are you—with courage.

The Courage to Be is about having the courage to be you: the genuine article. Having the Courage to Be yourself, is your opportunity to be free of external validation, no matter how wacky or quirky you may be.

We believe that there is a direct relationship between how little you care about what others might think and how much you have to offer the world around you.

Choose courage over conformity. Be you and enrich those around you rather than concealing your true self.

The alternative is sad—to waste your life hiding who you really are, literally hiding yourself from the world.

Without doubt, it takes more courage to be who you are than to be who you feel 'expected' to be. Mono-cultures are always looking for fresh followers, blank slates upon which to impress various values, goals and identities. What our homogenized, judgmental business world has come to recognize is that such cultures create a toxic work environment. Ongoing success requires more than something as nebulous as a culture—it takes individuals of outstanding courage coming together in common cause.

Conformity was crowned king and cowardice rewarded with managerial fiefdoms decades ago, but recently, castles have been toppled quite regularly. Why? Because the innovation required takes the Courage to Be—something which is often preached, yet so seldom practiced, especially in the workplace.

So many of us walk through life hiding behind masks. The price we pay? The ultimate price is a self-diluted life, weighted and masked by your fears of what others might think or what others might say. Even when present, we never really show up, let alone reveal ourselves. Known by many titles, but ultimately, anonymous. In the end, the name on the grave may be yours, but what of the epitaph?

More importantly, what of the alternative? What do we gain when we lose the mask? For those with the Courage to Be, the rewards are tremendous. When you choose to be your genuine self, you choose to live free of the common fears that define an external validated existence. In short, you get to be you at your best. When you do this, you tap into what makes you unique and that enriches far more than your life alone.

The Courage to Be (Is Not About You Alone)

Finding the Courage to Be understandably changes your life. It also enriches the lives of all those around you. Remember, courage is contagious, so for your own sake please stop concealing who you are and reveal yourself in all of your glory.

Also remember, we did not become courage coaches by innate virtue. Ross would be the first to admit that he spent too much of his life trying to be someone else and concealing his authentic self from life. Looking back on those years, he appreciates how much hard work went into maintaining that fiction.

That's true Bob. For much of my life a high percentage of my thoughts and feelings were focused on how I should be rather than just being. Now that I allow myself to be me, what I find is that life is just so much easier.

No mask is needed when there is nothing to hide, nor is there the incessant waste of personal energy. Now quite comfortable sharing openly, Ross has taken the deeper learning to heart and professional practice alike. Able to allow his true thoughts and feelings to shine through, Ross' world changed from one of 'concealing' to 'revealing' conversations.

The point is: courage came incrementally too, and has been worth every step.

Once you tap into that reservoir of courage within, you will discover that the genuine you has been there all along. The key to being you is to let go of the unreal you, the masked you, the artificial you. To do this you need only find the courage to listen to yourself rather than others.

One thing we know for certain is that it is impossible to be your authentic self when you are worried about impressing others and being popular.

A BRIEF EXERCISE

Who would you be if you no longer worried about what others might think or what others might say?

Who would you be if you no longer were trying to prove yourself to others or to be popular?

The answer to these two questions will point you to the genuine you.

To bring out of the best of what makes you unique is a gift to all of those around you. Why cheat others of your uniqueness? Face it, you can't really be anyone else anyway—only an imitation of a facsimile. Even if you are able to pull it off for some time, fatigue factor aside, what is the point?

By accessing the Courage to Be, you will no longer allow the opinions of others to determine who you are. You will chart your own path, be your own person and perhaps for the first time in your life, discover and reveal the unique gifts you possess.

In the words of Ralph Waldo Emerson, *"Every great man is unique."* We would hasten to add that such uniqueness lies within us all. The measure of the greatness may be known by many or few, but changes your life and the world around you.

Your Authentic Self Awaits

Our hope is that your experience is akin to our own. By letting go of your fears and need for external validation, you will allow yourself to discover the fullness of who you really are; to reveal your unique self to the world and embrace the liberating energies that flow when the person on the outside is the same as the person on the inside.

How do you do this? Quite simply, you employ courage to choose the "authentic you" over the "fake you" at every opportunity. Take a daily tally. Take courage, take your time and take the full measure of your progress. You will not be the only one to see your authentic self emerge. It may take a while, but simply by holding that choice in mind, you will become 100 per cent more you. You will have also gained a healthy dose of self-confidence and the respect of more than a few people.

In stepping up to the Courage to Be, those choices become a healthy set of reflex muscles—conditioned to reveal rather than conceal, to be genuine, to be real. The key to the first step of the *Ten Steps to Courage* is to stop giving your power away to whatever fears and anxieties have you reaching for that mask.

What do you have to gain? Yourself! As hard as it might be to imagine at present, makes for a world of difference. Simply put, the Courage to Be is all about stepping out and stepping up, from behind our masks and into the fullness of ourselves. Allowing ourselves to express our genuine being is liberating and takes us to a place of powerful freedom. The Courage to Be also gives us the ability to see the world differently, more truly. The unique talents of others become more readily apparent and an added dimension of appreciation and opportunity is added to the world.

So, what holds us back? What is it that we are afraid of? Is it ourselves? And if it is ourselves, what part of ourselves are we fearful of?

A BRIEF EXERCISE

What words would you use to describe the "authentic you"?

_____

What words would you use to describe the "fake you"?

_____

What behaviors do you need to walk away from to more fully become the authentic you?

_____

_____

What behaviors do you need to embrace to become the genuine you?

_____

_____

As you walk away from the person that you have become and walk towards the real you how do you feel? How will you and the world benefit from you becoming you?

_____

_____

_____

By accessing the courage to express your genuine self you

honour who you are meant to be. For all the riches in the world, there is nothing more liberating than being oneself.

It is so easy to be someone else other than yourself. It is easy to become the person who you are not. As a species, we learn by example. Blending in is easy, becoming part of the greater herd. We encourage you to get a 'moo-ve' on and get out of the gate. Especially in a world that seems to reward conformity, such 'cow'ardice no longer suits you.

To be vulnerable and to expose your true self will take plenty of courage. Do not be discouraged. The first step on any journey worth taking is always the most daunting. Daunts dwelled upon can haunt, so keep moving the peg towards your most authentic self daily.

The alternative is simply not worth dwelling upon for another day in your life. Every day spent being someone other than yourself is a day wasted—even if duly logged on the clock. You are doing yourself and the world a great disservice; you are denying both parties the most precious thing that you have to offer . . . yourself.

To be driven by what others might think or what others might say leaves us totally exposed to the sad state of conformity that restricts so many. Rather than succumbing to the culture of external validation, we encourage people to rise to an internally validated mode of living: wherein what you feel, think and do is in total sync with who you are. Be you. Be genuine.

Why do we think that the Courage to Be is so important that we have positioned it as the first of the Ten Steps to Courage? If we aren't able to find the Courage to Be ourselves, we can simply not hope to access the courage required to make an even greater difference.

The Courage to Dream

During coaching conversations, we often ask people, "What do you want your life to look like when you grow up?" We seldom receive a ready reply and in that silence is a sad truth. We have not been encouraged to dream.

This question is very different from the traditional, "What do you want to be when you grow up?" with its implication of occupation. We're interested in human beings. Our work should be a product of what we want our lives to look like. Our lives should not be defined by offered career paths alone. We all need the Courage to Dream.

Quite honestly, a lot of people don't know where they are headed beyond the daily parameters of home and work. As a result, they allow life to act upon them rather than actively engaging with their lives. It becomes an all too familiar life of trial and endurance. Questions of pursuing the life of their dreams and the life of their destiny are simply not asked.

The real danger of denying ourselves the Courage to Dream is that we end up with enduring someone else's nightmare and denying ourselves a far better life. A more mundane life amongst the walking, talking dead is no one's dream.

A BRIEF EXERCISE

Want to energize your life? You need to name your dream. You need to dream big. What do you really want your life to look like? When you ponder the possibilities how good could it be?

Why is it that people are hesitant to dream? We believe it boils down to a basic lack of courage and an inbred fear of failing. Failing is not failure. Not trying is failure. Sure dreaming is risky. The emotional risk of your dreams not coming true is real and common enough.

However, let's visit the alternative—a life in which dreams are smothered under layers of fear, doubt and rationalization. Where does that take you? All lives lead somewhere, however, not all destinations are desirable. We know you have the Courage to Dream of someplace far better.

Dreaming For Maximum Effect

In business, dreaming is most officially called strategic planning. The trouble is, while there is a whole lot of strategic planning in business, we see a failure to most truly dream big. Too often, strategic planning sessions are mired in a mindset of incremental metric growth as opposed to dreaming of a significant leap forward.

Without doubt, the Courage to Dream is a high stakes business. Its absence in the boardroom is a direct reflection of its absence in our daily lives. Think about it, corporations are ultimately people-powered and thereby dream-driven—or left to idle. For all the talk of innovation and next level solutions, the Courage to Dream is a prerequisite we need afford ourselves.

Imagine what your future might look like if you followed your dreams? For those who choose to do so, the future is bright. For those who choose to let tomorrow come, stasis is inevitable. Bewilderingly, the numbers of those that move beyond the state of self-imposed petrification are rare.

We encourage you to bring dreaming back into your life so that you will enhance the meaningfulness of the life you live. After all, you only have one life. What do you want it to look like?

Another way of thinking about the unwillingness to dream

is to think about the price you pay if you choose not to dream. What does the absence of dreaming cost you in your life? What is it that you are giving up by choosing not to dream? By aiming low in life what will your life look like? What will you be missing out on?

While some people feel uncomfortable with the word "dream" there is a specific reason that we use it rather than 'plan' or something similarly mundane.

To dream is to be emotionally connected to that which makes our hearts sing. As such, it is something that pre-exists the workplace and strategic planning sessions alike. When dream and vocation align, the successes that manifest are both effortless and entirely natural.

Showing up to a strategic planning session is expected. We encourage the unexpected: share a dream. The results often prove priceless at both work and in the bigger picture.

The trouble is simply filling a seat and following order on the agenda does not inspire anyone—nor does it bring your dreams any closer to reality. Plus, it gets boring, but then so does the rest of life without the Courage to Dream.

Rather than enduring this malaise or worse yet, growing increasingly resigned towards life, the establishment, et al., ask yourself, "Can I dream of a better life?"

We all can. To give them voice takes the Courage to Dream aloud. If that dream calls upon the skills and initiatives of others, sharing is everything. Once in pursuit of a shared dream, life and bottom lines alike benefit from a vast pool of positive emotion. This is another reason to dream big and take aim at your most authentic self and target alike—exciting dreams produce exciting lives.

Everything is Created Twice (First in Our Dreams)

Stephen Covey tells us that everything is created twice. First in our dreams and then in reality. The benefits of dreaming are both huge and immediate.

First of all, once you have a dream or destination in sight you will be propelled towards it. Your life will become more meaningful.

Secondly, you will no longer settle for what life brings you, but reach for and ask for more from life. In life, you don't get what you deserve but rather you get what you ask for and aspire for. *"If you can't name it, then you can't claim it"* are Dr. Phil's wise words. If we don't know what we want, we can't even ask for it.

Thirdly, when your dream finds a home in the heads and hearts of others, a special flow of energy is created in all aspects of your life. It is as if you are plugged into a special power source available only to dreamers.

Visualization, filling out the details, is key to the process of dreaming effectively. Once you possess a crystal clear understanding of your dream and what you want your life to look like, you will be amazed at the bridges that appear and the doors that will open. The truth is the Courage to Dream will take you to places you never thought imaginable.

Stop playing it small or not at all. Don't let the anxieties, uncertainties and fear of the future get in the way of your dreams. Playing it small boils down to avoidance: avoiding risk, failure and criticism. We often call this playing it safe, but playing it small is dangerous in long and short runs alike.

If you are going to let what others might think of your dreams keep you from bringing them forward in the first place, reality will never benefit from your dreams—and neither will you. It's a good thought to tuck into your head before you clear your mind and go to sleep.

The Hippo in the Campus (A Nod to Napping)

In fact, did you know that research tells us that deep sleep, dreaming and daydreaming helps us plan better for the future?

In a recent study, people who took naps in which they achieved deep REM (rapid eye movement) sleep—wherein dreams are most vivid—performed better on creativity-oriented word problems. According to the psychiatrists who led the study, REM sleep helps people combine ideas in new ways, and improved participants' ability to see connections among seemingly unrelated things.

Furthermore, sleep actually helps people turn their memories into predictions. Boosted by deep sleep, an improved memory and cognitive connectedness has one definite benefit: helping you imagine and better plan for the future.

"When you imagine future events, you're recombining aspects of experiences that have actually occurred," says Harvard psychiatrist Dr. Daniel Schacter. Dr. Schacter has found that the same areas in the brain that handle memory, such as the hippocampus, show increased activity when subjects are asked to imagine future events.

Do we become crystal balls in REM sleep? The possibility exists. Dr. Schatcher "suspects there might be a connection. After all, dreams are a different way of recombining aspects of past experience."

According to a Harvard study of 2,250 volunteers by psychologists Daniel Gilbert and Matthew Killingsworth, our minds are wandering for 47 per cent of the time we are awake. Whether this is a bad thing is worth considering.

At first glance, the data seems like a confirmation of our inherent laziness, but that is due to the inherently negative perception of daydreaming. In a work culture obsessed with efficiency, the wandering-mind is derided as an organizational drain. This is by no means a modern devaluation alone. Freud, for instance, described daydreams as "infantile" and a means of escaping from the necessary chores of the world into fantasy.

However, in recent years psychologists and neuroscientists have rethought the value of daydreaming, revealing it to be a quite essential cognitive tool. It turns out that whenever we are slightly bored, when reality isn't quite enough to keep us occupied, our minds turn to other scenarios. We begin exploring our own associations, contemplating connections not always apparent when our focus is attuned to any given task. In this light, our daydreams serve a similar function as our sleeping dreams and facilitate bursts of creative energy and insight.

The bottom line is that there is a direct relationship between daydreaming and creativity. Those that are more prone to daydreaming are likely to be better at generating new ideas.

A paper published by the neuroscientists Dr. Wagner and Dr. Born demonstrates the power of dreaming. The researchers gave a group of students a tedious task with a simple solution—transforming a long list of number strings into a new set of number strings. Wagner and Born designed the task with a shortcut that might only be discovered by subject insight. Less than 20 of the participants found the shortcut, even when left to their own devices for several hours to think over the task. Instead, the vast majority spent that time over thinking the task.

That was before nap time. In follow up research Harvard psychologists Dr. Gilbert and Dr. Killingsworth allowed the participants to take a nap. The act of dreaming during the nap changed everything that happened thereafter. After people were allowed to slip into REM sleep, nearly 60 per cent of them discovered the secret pattern. By allowing the participants to sink into REM sleep, Gilbert and Killingsworth produced results that were 300 per cent greater than those produced by hours of hard thinking and effort.

Could it be that sleeping, dreaming and daydreaming are the foundation of genius?

If this all sounds like scientific justification for afternoon naps and long showers—you are right. We have always assumed that paying attention to solving the problem allowed a person to get more done. Perhaps the opposite is true. Rather than forcing the mind to solve the problem, the likelihood of success is enhanced when you dream a little dream—be it day or night.

A daydream is just a means of tapping into those fresh thoughts generated by our unconscious. Others, even ourselves, may think that we are wasting time, while in reality a highly intellectual fountain of creative solution is surging to the surface.

So for all of you daydreamers out there . . . keep dreaming.

Everything is created twice. First in our heads and then in reality. If we deny ourselves the opportunity to daydream then we will never have the vision to convert to reality.

So if you were to discover the Courage to Dream, what would your dream look like?

The Courage to Trust

Trust is a very deep and interesting topic. We agree that trust must exist in any healthy relationship. We also hear people talk about how a "healthy amount of distrust" is requisite in business as a precautionary measure. And we wonder why so many people have issues with trust in the workplace?

We believe that a critical component of developing the Courage to Trust lies in remembering that people are people—all of us.

From time to time, people make mistakes in judgment and succumb to either fear or temptation. Here's where the Courage to Trust becomes something of a judgement call, in that it is yours alone to make both in work and in life. Consider your partner in either. How resilient to temptation is your partner? How well equipped are they to avoid mistakes? What values guide their moral compass?

A BRIEF EXERCISE

List the five qualities you look for in a trustworthy person.

1. _____

2. _____

3. _____

4. _____

5. _____

Do you display the five qualities you look for in a trustworthy person? If not, why not?

_____

_____

_____

List five names of people you trust and why.

1. _____

2. _____

3. _____

4. _____

5. _____

List five reasons to be more trusting.

1. _____

2. _____

3. _____

4. _____

5. _____

Trust is simply another word for comfort.

"How comfortable am I with this person?" The answer will determine how much we are willing to risk, be it in terms of money, reputation, time or our emotions.

We also think trust, communication and expectation are very closely aligned. We can't count the number of times we have felt betrayed or disappointed because our expectations of a relationship (personal or professional) were not shared by the other party.

Trust thrives best when communication is crystal clear, boundaries are set and all parties have an equal and mutual respect for each other. It also seems to work best when everyone has "skin in the game," in other words something to win or lose. This seems to serve as an incentive to remain "trustworthy."

Personally, it disappoints us to think trust requires incentive. This puts concepts of benevolence and honour outside the scope of the boardroom, to say nothing of the Courage to Trust. We need not have something tangible to lose before we call upon the Courage to Trust—and in turn be trusted.

The Courage to Trust often feels more like the courage to risk and seek the innate worth in every person. To trust in the absence of knowing whether someone is worthy of trust, requires a leap of faith, an innate acceptance grounded in what feels right. This brings us into the realm of the "gut feel" and first impressions.

We consider trust a mix of applied intellect and intuitive decision-making.

It's also important to remember that trust is a two-way

street. This requires some introspection to evaluate our own trustworthiness. Here is where we need to be the most courageous and honest with ourselves.

A BRIEF EXERCISE

Am I worthy of your trust?   Yes   No

Will I act in an honourable fashion?   Yes   No

Will I have my partner's best interest at heart as well as my own?   Yes   No

Do I trust myself not to succumb to temptation?   Yes   No

Have I been honest in my assessment of my ability to avoid mistakes?   Yes   No

Am I capable of "doing the job"?   Yes   No

If we can answer all of the above with a definitive "Yes," then and only then can we consider the Courage to Trust others.

The last thought we have about trust involves how one manages disappointment. We hear people say things like "I am so disappointed. I trusted him to come through for me" or "she really let me down. I was counting on her to . . ."

Disappointment is a normal occurrence, so we need to deal with it constructively. Otherwise, that which crushes us can become a crutch, a precedent denying all future attempts.

We also think that the word trust can become a crutch—and a crippling one if wielded or yielded without courage. Trusting blindly or to secure external validation is as foolish as dreaming small. Similarly, 'trusting' someone else to do something, how readily do we find fault when things don't work as well as hoped.

"It's not my fault that they were incompetent!"

"It's not my fault that they fell to temptation!"

"It's not my fault that their moral compass was broken!"

If the above sounds like a 'grown-up' version of Billy from the Family Circus cartoons, you have just hit upon the real reason for that cartoon's longevity. There's more than a bit of the "Not Me" in all of us—until we grow the ability of others to trust in us.

As we said, trust is a very deep and interesting topic.

The Courage to Act

> "Action is a great restorer and builder of confidence. Inaction is not only the result, but the cause, of fear. Perhaps the action you take will be successful; perhaps different action or adjustments will have to follow. But any action is better than no action at all."
> —Norman Vincent Peale

If there is one thing that we have learned on our own journey it is this: life rewards action and seriously and significantly penalizes inaction.

Now that you have found the Courage to Be, Dream and Trust, the next step is to cultivate the Courage to Act. Courage is the catalytic converter of your dreams. Activated in noble purpose, it converts your dreams into reality.

The best way to achieve your intentions is to provide them with the necessary attention. We said it earlier, your intentions need attention. A dream is only that if not acted upon.

What is it that stops us from finding the Courage to Act? For starters, rather than telling ourselves the right stuff, we tend to tune into just the opposite. Then there is the fact that so much of our inaction is justified by fear. The time has come to take your fear apart and see it for what it is—**F**alse **E**xpectations **A**ppearing **R**eal.

We love the acronym for fear. Isn't it so true? In the words of Mark Twain, *"I am an old man and have known a great many troubles, but most of them never happened."*

In sports it's called 'psyching ourselves out.'

Not only do we tell ourselves the wrong stories, we are drawn to the darkest imaginings our mind can conjure to stop us from taking action. We have all frozen at the foul line. We are paralyzed as these negative thoughts consume our minds and we can think of nothing other than what people are going to say or what people are going to think when . . . not if . . . we fail.

Do not fall prey to the negative tapes of self-doubt that pollute our minds. We are about to not only face fear, but also act in the face of fear.

First of all let's get real. No matter what your dream may be, what is the worst thing that is going to happen to you? Is someone going to shoot you? Of course not. What we are really talking about is not fear as often as a degree of anxiety—either in a spot or on the spot.

Whenever either of us are at that spot, we recognize it for what it is—an excellent opportunity for us to activate the Courage to Act.

From Dreams Into Actions

Of course, actions without steps work up a sweat, but rarely fulfill dreams. It can seem overwhelming when we review the list of actions required to make our dreams a reality. As a result, too few find the Courage to Act effectively upon those things that would make the greatest difference at both work and home.

Our suggestions to achieving your dreams are simple. First of all, compile a list of the actions needed to achieve your dream. List them in a chronological sequence.

Now get started on the first action item. It's not a complicated process, but it does take courage. You now see why courage is integral to so much potential in our lives.

Finding the Courage to Act, to just get started and out of the gate, is often the most difficult step. Once you are on your way, momentum will build and carry you, your dream and a great many others, a vast distance. That said, those first few steps can feel like an eternity. To us it is about just getting started.

You may not be totally aware of all of the steps necessary to achieving your dream. That need not hold you back. You have the trajectory of where you are headed. You have your dream, a solid outline and momentum is beginning to build from your initial actions. The dream is in action.

Typically, when people think of the Courage to Act, the heroic feats of Hollywood actors on the big screen spring to mind. That's acting. It's also a passive experience. It is nothing but watching a movie. The Courage to Act is about you! The truth is that the real Courage to Act is a more internal, character driven-accomplishment. Look away from the external drama. Seek within. Act. Your courage will grow.

There are two things that you need to do if you are to successfully act on your dream. The first is to assign a time line to your actions. Commit to achieving specific goals by a specific time. The second thing you need to do is tell people about your intentions. As long as you keep it a secret the odds of it happening decrease significantly. Both of these ideas work well for us and are instrumental in helping us get out of the gate daily in pursuit of our dreams.

A BRIEF EXERCISE

For your dream what are the actions that you need to take?

_____

_____

_____

What is the chronological order of these actions?

_____

_____

_____

For the first action, when do you commit to getting started and completing it?

_____

_____

_____

And there you go. You are in action.

Is it really that simple? Yes, it is. When you are armed with the realization that the only things stopping you are the self-limiting stories swirling through your mind raising alarms, the facade of your fears drops. It is simply noise. Do you want your life to be stunted as a result of the noise?

We think the folks at Nike have it right when they say, *"Feel the fear and do it anyways."* Our only concern with this statement is that we are really giving our power away to what we are calling fear. We empower too much negativity by giving the name 'fear' too much of the discomfort in our lives. As discussed, most of our mountains are molehills made enormous in our minds.

A BRIEF EXERCISE

List three actions you want to take immediately.

1. _____

2. _____

3. _____

For each action list three things that are stopping you.

1. _____

2. _____

3. _____

For each action list all the rewards that would result in taking the action

1. _____

2. _____

3. _____

For each obstacle list what is required to overcome that obstacle.

_____

_____

_____

Often we hear from people who say that they wouldn't feel comfortable doing this or doing that. In many cases, neither would we, but we encourage them to push ahead. We would not let our own fears bring our lives to a screeching halt, nor could we ignore the likely opportunity for growth.

The funny thing about acting in the face of what we call fear is how easy it is to walk through our self-created walls and emerge unscarred. That awakened realization helps us as we continue to grow our courage. Employ the Courage to Act to overcome any obstacle and share the rewards.

The Courage to Listen

> "If you are talking, all you are doing is repeating something you already know. If you listen, you might learn something new."
>
> —J. P. McEvoy

Listening is difficult for most people. As humans, we have developed a great need to be heard. Yet, we do very little in the way of listening. The Courage to Listen requires particular attention given how little of our communication needs to be face-to-face in the modern context.

Think about the last time you were in a conversation with someone. Were you really listening? Maybe you were making eye contact. Perhaps you were nodding in agreement. But were you really listening?

The Courage to Listen is not a thing of half measures and may be the greatest gift we have to offer each other.

Let's be honest. A lot of the time, we are not listening, or even half-listening, but thinking about what we are going to say next. When our brain is engaged in formulating our next brilliant salvo of words designed to disarm our conversational opponent, we hear ourselves alone. We are so concerned with being heard that we totally sacrifice the information coming to us.

Don't feel too bad, the other person is likely doing the same thing! As a result the essence of the communication is lost, yet both might consider their communications clearly and concisely delivered. True to a point—if only anyone was listening.

Might this need to be heard stem directly from a fear of

what we might hear if we listened? Living in fear of greater truths, we go to great ends to ensure we rarely hear what people are saying.

None of us wants to hear what we hold to be true is not. Greater truths take uncommon courage. The more greatly we hold something to be true, the more we need to draw upon the Courage to Listen.

What is the worst that might result from having your mind changed? All of us can be brighter. We have all been owed an apology. Some of us may even have received an apology. It makes for good conversation. There is nothing to fear in any of this.

If the greatest fear in the world is the opinion of someone else, the good news is you are now familiar with the antidote to this sorry situation. The moment you find the courage to both listen and step beyond diverging opinion, you are transformed. You are no longer a sheep in a herd, but a lion roaming free—or whatever you choose to be.

Isn't it amazing how the opinions of others can traumatize us? Merely thoughts and words, yet empowered by our own fears, capable of triggering our most prehistoric decision-making process—'fight or flight.' It might have been a while since a saber-toothed tiger mistook us for supper, but human history has given the limbic system plenty of reason to keep fit since. Good to know the safety gear is still working, but how much does it dampen our true perception of life's opportunities? Do the opinions of others really equate with a saber-toothed tiger?

Are we really so frightened of what others might say that we chose to deny them our ability to listen? Information flows back and forth, but ultimately amounts to a null exchange.

Two Ears, One Mouth: A Ratio with Reason

Communication is the missing keyword and keystone of the Courage to Listen. Courageous communications makes fine math of proper manners. Two ears, two eyes and one mouth: a ratio offered with reason. We firmly believe you need to earn the right to be heard in any conversation. Fortunately, that is easily done by first listening.

When you have the Courage to Listen to others and really hear what they are saying, you are hearing 'their' truth. Everyone is not only entitled to their truth—it is inevitable until we learn otherwise. Then again, some of what you hear will have less to offer. There is a little catch phrase that you can silently add to the statements of others in those cases. "In your opinion."

Communication is a two-way street. When we have the Courage to Listen and truly hear another, we gain a deeper insight into what makes us each unique and what connects us.

We are all so very different. We come from different places. We have had a world of varying experiences. How could our thoughts and perspectives be anything but as varied as they are? Why then do we so often expect people to think just like we do?

Rather than rejecting the opinions of others, we need to courageously listen to them and when you hear the opinions of others you will become more respectful of their perspective.

We don't believe it is necessary to agree upon the world as it is. Instead, we need the courage to see the world as we are—and as shown to be by others. Our lens of perspective need be neither static nor singular. With the Courage to Listen, the world evolves daily from this most incredible of common gifts.

How much courage does it really take to stop moving our lips and actually enjoying the benefits of what others have to say? There is a reward in such imposed silencing of our need to be heard. You just might hear something new, something that will shift your perspective, give you new insight—or get you out of a gate you never knew existed.

Don't Judge. Hear. Listen.
When coaching others, we are consistently inspired by some pretty great stories. What has always amazed us is how often the real gems come from some of the most unassuming people in the room. And the surprise has not been ours alone. Those most likely to be voted least likely to contribute meaningful ideas seem to have an innate propensity to surprise the most jaded workshop veteran. Repeatedly, we have been wowed with incredible insights from the most unlikely places.

What have we learned? Don't judge. Hear. Listen.

There is a difference between listening and hearing isn't there?

For many, listening is what they do whenever their lips are not moving. Inaction does not equate input received. Not good enough. We have heard this referred to as 'lock and load' listening. The lips may not be moving, but is listening the focus? No. It is simply a reload for the next volley.

Real listening means you are courageously hearing both words and deeper meaning alike. It requires a few more mental muscles too. Once mastered, the Courage to Listen silences our automatic response systems, and allows us to hear with optimal clarity.

Listening to Our Inner Self
While the Courage to Listen can test our limbic system and patience at times, there is another act of aural sympathy needed.

We need the Courage to Listen to our inner self. Alright, so maybe we all understand that on an innate level already.

We hear the truth, but it falls on d'fears? In the absence of courage, solutions are always sought elsewhere, until we know where to look and how to hear our inner self.

We encourage you to listen to your inner self. Over the years we have become so scientifically-orientated, too often we discount our inner self. We tend to rely on the opinions of others to such a degree that we have forgotten that our inner self even exists.

When we do, we give it little validity and choose to depend on others rather than ourselves. When we don't even trust our own thoughts, we have truly become addicted to the opinions of others. We need to go deep inside ourselves to hear what our inner selves have to say. Our experience has been that when we find the courage to listen to ourselves we will often find the answers to questions we had not even considered! So go on, have a little chat with yourself. It's not crazy. In fact, it is required!

A BRIEF EXERCISE

Find a quiet place and take some time to identify a topic that you would want to chat to yourself about.

Start the conversation by asking yourself a question related to that topic. Then shut up and listen. Write down the result of your conversation as reference. Repeat this exercise often. It is one of the most powerful problem solving skills you can acquire.

The Courage to Tolerate

No contradiction here, but the Courage to Tolerate is confusing at first glance—and challenging thereafter! The thrust of this is quite simple though. Sometimes it is wise to exercise restraint over immediate action.

To live with courage and confidence is a great thing. However, it can also be intoxicating without suitable safeguards. Like most things in life, confidence without control can become an unwieldy and double-edged blade. The Courage to Tolerate is the key to such control.

Imagine how conflict-filled life would become if you felt compelled to take cause against everything with which you disagreed. Countering every differing opinion, correcting every error, leading every discussion: ridiculous and exhausting? We have met too many people just like this in our lives. Generally speaking, they are exhausted, lonely and confused as to why the world is so argumentative.

It's as important to develop and manage your emotional and rational "filters" as it is to retrain your brain to escape the "fight or flight" knee jerk reactions to life's challenges. This is the process wherein you decide whether or not it is worth going to battle on an issue that affects you. These filters play a multi-dimensional role in keeping you from going crazy or, worse yet, doing things you might regret later.

For starters, your filters give you time to process what you are feeling, seeing and hearing. Why is this important? Well, it provides the time required to assess the situation, order your emotions and decide whether or not you are willing to adjust your perspective or stand primed to defend the one you hold. For all intents and purposes, your filters buy you time to respond appropriately.

Passion is a good thing. Blind passion is not. Neither does every action require a reaction. The Courage to Tolerate builds directly upon the Courage to Listen and allows you to decide whether your emotions are challenging your ability to do either. So often we dis-engage our intellect and leave our emotions unchecked and this can lead to taking actions based on simply how we feel without giving it any thought!

Ultimately, the Courage to Tolerate is gained when the causes you do choose to champion are those well worth the effort. Your filters help you make these determinations and save you from what would be relentless frustration.

The Backbone of a Free Society

Tolerance is a significant factor in our society and the backbone of any free society. It is also hotly debated in many circles. Tolerance places its demands on both sides of all equations—and rarely are there only two sides. Nor is it always easy, as tolerance is almost exclusively called upon in conflict situations large and small.

For the most part, North American society embraces tolerance—except when we disagree with each other, which of course happens daily. Nonetheless, our well-developed filters allow us to believe what we want, say what we want and in many cases do what we want to do with our lives—without going to war to either defend our views or change the views of those with a different perspective. Tolerance also allows us to engage in respectful and thoughtful debate and keeps us away from shouting matches. Well, most of the time.

In order for anyone to be free to speak their mind, someone else who disagrees with them has to be tolerant of their message in order to be able to say what they think. Simple, right? Yet in some countries you can be shot for saying what you think.

This ability to tolerate others is not static; there is no on and off switch. Instead, tolerance comes in varying degrees, akin to elastic bands.

For example, you might have a roommate or a family member who likes to play loud music. You don't like loud music, but are willing to stretch your tolerance for a while because you see how much they are enjoying it. Now though, it's getting late. You feel your tolerance being stretched tightly. The loud music continues—even after offering visual cues through body language and facial expression involving much yawning and eye-rubbing. Much like the rubber band, your tolerance snaps. You take action and ask that the music be turned down.

You might have asked at any time. You might have snapped at any time. Instead, with the Courage to Tolerate you let the loud music play, asked politely and regained the quiet of your home. You also avoided an unneeded conflict.

Your internal filters helps you to determine whether or not you are willing to tolerate any given situation, and thereafter gauge how much tolerance you have for any particular behavior. The balance is delicate. On one hand, if you have no tolerance for anything, it is likely that you will be ostracized. You will simply not be able to fit into society regardless of whether or not you are right if you disagree with everyone involved.

On the other hand, if your capacity for tolerance is immense, it is likely that you will be consistently taken advantage of and you will not experience the sense of free will that is afforded to others. If you simply go along with whatever, or whoever is in control, your life is not your own. Moreover, you will be regarded as untrustworthy if you cannot stand up for something or someone in life.

These extremes are rare, but they help us understand the need to employ tolerance appropriately. It also causes us to consider the need for good judgment. If everyone had a handle on this concept, this book would not be necessary. However, it is often too easy to expand tolerance, and forego the courage to say "enough is enough."

The Courage to Act calls upon action. The Courage to Tolerate calls upon our inner calm. Yet, as with all of the 10 Steps to Courageous Living, they are connected. Tolerance is not passive and should never be confused with "going with the flow."

The path of least resistance is too often rife with the intolerances of others. Yet when tolerance is abused, stretched beyond its natural limits, this creates stress, disappointment and resentment. It can often result in less than objective judgement and actions which give later cause to regret.

A BRIEF EXERCISE

Write down three recent examples of when you feel you were "tolerant" and why you think you chose tolerance over action.

1. _____

2. _____

3. _____

Was this level of tolerance appropriate? What if anything would you do differently?

Write down three recent examples of when you feel you were less than "tolerant" and why you chose action over tolerance.

1. _____

2. _____

3. _____

Was this level of intolerance appropriate? What if anything would you do differently?

This exercise will help you develop your judgement skill reflexes and clarify your personal tolerance levels. In other words, it will help you to "pick your battles."

The Courage to Reflect

Garcia the Spanish philosopher tells us that *"Reflection is truly the school of all wisdom."*

Ah, another great quote from the ages. The one gift that age has given us is experience. What we all learn in time is that experience can only be translated into wisdom if we summon the Courage to Reflect.

To us reflection is our ability and willingness to look within ourselves and learn. Ross considers himself blessed in that he has a little cabin tucked away in the mountains. No phone. No electricity. No disruptions. It is in this silence, serenity and solitude that he has learned much from reflection.

Ross's cabin is a very special place for him. He is consistently amazed what self-reflection in the wilderness has enabled him to unearth and understand about his thoughts and actions. Like many of us Ross tends to beat himself up every time he finds himself as less than the ideal he holds for himself. Having a place and space to face those kinds of feelings is important. If you are going to be rigorously and perhaps even ruthlessly honest with yourself, you need a healthy dose of courage to accept and meet what shows up. We encourage you to find that place in the world where you can be alone with your thoughts from time to time without distraction. You will be amazed with what you will find there.

Currently one of the national banks is running an ad that declares that you are, "Richer than you think." We don't know about that, but with The Courage to Reflect you are certain to be wealthier. Every one of us has accumulated a wealth of wisdom. In order to access it we need to find the Courage to Reflect on our lives and live up to the lessons we have learned.

For both the authors of this book, that happens most easily when we get away from the everyday. Only when we are able to immerse ourselves in the silence of nature are we fully able to engage in meaningful self-reflection. It may be the forest. It may be a rooftop. Wherever your zone of reflection finds you, it leads to further reaches within.

Once you are in your zone of reflection you will be amazed what shows up. Lessons and wisdoms appear that will reveal truths and take you places that you never thought possible. With the Courage to Reflect, we step back to step forward and assess to aspire to greater courage yet.

If you aren't looking into yourself, chances are you're not helping anyone, yourself included—definitely not to the extent that might make a real difference. Without the Courage to Reflect, big pictures escape us and the small things we might do to improve them never rise to the surface. When we reflect one thing becomes obvious—none of us are right all of the time. It takes courage, a whopping dose of courage, to admit you are wrong and own it. Amazing things often happen when we do.

Being reflective is not covered off by gazing into the mirror. Your reflection has little to do with your inner-self. "Mirror, mirror on the wall," is how it goes for those who reflect only upon the external and see no opportunity for themselves to learn and grow.

In our jam-packed lives we leave little time for reflection. Little time to look back and to learn. Our failure to do so cheats us of our accumulated wisdom's true worth.

Is it easy to look back and reflect on our behaviors and our feelings? Of course not, but while dreams and actions might change the immediate state of our lives, reflection raises the bar on another level, enhancing the overall quality of our lives.

We recognize that over the last decade our lives have become busier and busier. Focused on the pressures of survival, we have drawn away from reflection. In the absence of reflection, we act on impulse, as if on auto-pilot, repeating past responses without consideration of alternative. We are doing rather than being.

Seneca, the ancient Roman hero encouraged those seeking knowledge of the self to, *"Be harsh with yourself at times."* Those times called upon tougher stock, so let's swap harsh for honest and enduring.

Indeed, we are not laying siege upon ourselves so much as taking a hard line with a soft approach. We need the Courage to Reflect in order to both quiet the mind and mine the full potential of its acquired wisdoms.

James Allen suggests that *"Only by much searching and mining are gold and diamonds obtained, and man can find every truth connected with his being if he will dig deep into the mine of his soul."*

So many of us have lost sight of our inner selves, our true selves. We encourage you to go to the wilderness, sit on a rock or drop down onto the soil. Sink deep into your soul and the Courage to Reflect will find you.

A BRIEF EXERCISE

Take a moment to identify a place in your daily life where you can be at peace and is silent and void of all distraction.

Schedule time to go to this place and answer to yourself the following questions.

Who am I?

Where have I been?

What have I learned?

What makes me happy?

Where am I going?

Be courageous and welcome the answers. If you don't like what you hear, be courageous and take appropriate actions towards change. Remember, be honest with yourself. It inspires the best in all others.

The Courage to Speak Up

We don't know about you but for us, we have spent way too much of our lives not speaking up; not speaking our truths. The Courage to Speak Up is a theme that lies near and dear to the hearts of anyone who has ever been afflicted by FOSU. What is FOSU? Fear of Speaking Up.

FOSU is a cancer that rots at the souls of our lives, our families, our workplaces and our nations. We are reminded of the Pogo quote from the 1970s, "I have seen the enemy, and he is us." The price we pay for not speaking up is monumental.

No one says it better than Rabbi Prenz, a German Jew serving in Germany during the reign of Hitler: *"When I was the rabbi of the Jewish community in Berlin under the Hitler regime, I learned many things. The most important thing that I learned under those tragic circumstances was that bigotry and hatred are not the most urgent problem. The most urgent, the most disgraceful, the most shameful and the most tragic problem is silence."*

Prenz went on to become the President of the World Jewish Congress and a Leader in the American Civil Rights Movement. Read his last sentence again.

"The most urgent, the most disgraceful, the most shameful and the most tragic problem is silence."

What does this mean to you? To what degree does this relate to how you live your life?

Do you want to be outrageously courageous and immediately receive a free pass to The Hall of Courage? Speak up! Some may classify it as going rogue. We consider you an active agent of better things to come.

If you think it . . . say it!

How often have you sat with a spouse, a friend, a colleague at work or a boss and did exactly the opposite? Exactly. If you are like most people the truthful answer to this question is, "far too often."

Too many people wait their entire lives to speak up. Few do so without regret. In fact, a recent "death bed" study asked people facing life's end what regrets weighed most heavily upon them. Not surprisingly, the top three regrets centered around courage.

1. They regret that they did not have the courage to be themselves and live the life they wanted rather than living the life that others expected of them.

2. They regret that they did not have the courage to say what they really meant.

3. They regret that they did not have the courage to work less and enhance the quality of their lives.

Each of the above is a comment on the choices we make that become our lives. In each case, their regrets were rooted in lives fueled by fear. What did they fear? Primarily the same thing we have discussed throughout this book. They feared what others would think about them or say about them.

A BRIEF EXERCISE

Consider the greatest truth you might share with another. Think of how the first 20 seconds would sound if you had the Courage to Speak Up. Write it down.

Where do you think the 20 seconds of insane courage you

just practiced will take you? To freedom. Once you are 20 seconds into whatever needs to be said you will find that you have the courage and momentum to continue.

Our experience is that only with the Courage to Speak Up are you able to make each day really count. Showing up is a good start. Speaking up is great. If we are not making each day count by showing up then we are simply counting days.

When we self-censor our expression we are really killing a big part of who we are—what are we telling ourselves about our own level of self-esteem?

By not speaking up we are not only imposing a frightening level of self-censure, but setting ourselves up to be oppressed. We are all too familiar with the "Oh, woe is me" crowd, those who continuously choose fear over courage and say nothing. If they do say anything, it is typically what we call a "concealing" rather than a "revealing" conversation.

Concealing conversations are what we engage in so much of the time. We never really say what we mean, do we? In fact for many of us in business, and in all aspects of life, the real message often is in what is not said as much as the words actually spoken.

The truth is that when we practice this form of self-censure we are harmed by our decision to silently comply. The trouble is, the more we repress our feelings, the magnitude of stress, anxiety and frustration grows. Want to remove a ton of stress from your life? Stop stuffing your thoughts away and speak up! What is the worst thing that can happen if you develop the Courage to Speak Up and state your opinion?

A BRIEF EXERCISE

Here's a way to prepare for the next time you are in this position of opportunity.

Remain calm. If your emotions are too heightened you will likely not communicate your thought or position well.

Start by saying, "Here's what I think . . ." This shows ownership of communication and positions the statement as a declaration—not an offer to be debated, but a declaration of what you hold to be true.

Once you have made your statement, stop speaking. You are under no obligation to apologize for what you think. You are under no obligation to defend what you think.

If someone else brings more information to the discussion that causes you to reassess your position, that's fine, but you are under no obligation to adopt someone else's point of view. Just remember, they are under no obligation to adopt yours either.

It is amazing what can be achieved if "all the cards are on the table." Give yourself the permission to courageously speak what's on your mind.

The Courage to Say No

No, reading this book will not give you courage—only you can do that. Much depends upon two simple letters that challenge us all—no.

Clearly, we understand that saying "no" takes courage. Hearing it can be challenging too! This is why we struggle with decisions. In so many cases, the decision-process is secondary to finding the Courage to Say No.

Knowing how and when to say no and when to summon the Courage to Tolerate is a matter of making the most of your actions. In business, we find too many people prepared to compromise in agreement and the result is a culture of mediocrity. Decision-making en masse may seem a safe and unified gesture, but it serves no one well.

It is only when you speak up, and most often when you say no, that mediocrity gives way to greatness. After all, a measure of conflict and critical opinion is key to all innovation!

While this is familiar thinking to any and all entrepreneurs, it is also why the world has so many more employees than entrepreneurs. We know that the risks of the entrepreneurial life requires a depth of courage that few seem willing to access or exercise. Making decisions is easy—in our heads! Fortunately, that is where we must first find all forms of courage. The Courage to Say No to options that are not the best for you can only help liberate the decision-making processes of others.

By saying no you give yourself the opportunity to walk away from the clutter and noise of the wrong things and clearly see the right things.

So let us ask you this. Do you have the Courage to Say No to the things that have brought fear into your life most often? In this case, we sincerely hope you have the Courage to Say YES!

Just say yes, but then consider how often we simply agree to avoid disagreeing. Is this why so many people are stressed out these days? We say yes to everything and in doing so clutter our lives with activities that don't make our hearts sing. Yes, we may be busy, but is our goal to simply be busy?

No. Being busy is just an addiction to activity.

If you want to be successful in all aspects of your life you need to start saying no to the wrong things. It is only then that you are able to say yes to the right things.

Ross was recently talking with one of his son's friends, a young man in his twenties who owns a software development firm. Ross was impressed with how this young entrepreneur had already gained the Courage to Reflect on his early years in business. He had learned the true value of saying no to anything that was not a great fit for him. The Courage to Say No had allowed him to create a clear path and direction for himself and his colleagues.

As he explained to Ross, his belief in the Courage to Say No allowed him to grow the success of his firm by focusing time and energy on the right things and not allowing others to dilute his dreams. Ross was very impressed to hear such wisdom from such a young individual. It spoke volumes of the essentially ageless beauty of courage.

A BRIEF EXERCISE

Write down three recent instances where you said Yes when you wanted to say No.

_____

_____

_____

List the reasons for doing so:

_____

_____

_____

Are any of the reasons rational? Are any of the reasons fear based?

_____

_____

_____

If you had said no, would any of the consequences resulted in harm to you or anyone else?

_____

_____

_____

It is important to remember that saying "no" to something that is wrong or clearly isn't in your best interest is a reasonable and rational thing to do. What is also amazing is that after you practice this a few times, people come to know you as a person who can't be taken advantage of, and the frequency of such decisions dwindle away. On the other hand, the more often you say "yes" to something that is either wrong or clearly not in your best interest, the more you will be targeted.

Finding the courage to say "no" will give you strength, boost your self-esteem, keep you out of trouble and it gets easier to do as you work towards a sense of fearlessness.

The Courage to Adapt

While this book directly targets the courage deficit, we are not without our inspirations. We are constantly amazed at the depth of courage some people have developed to function and maintain a positive outlook in today's society.

Courage and change are complementary cousins, the first giving us what is fundamentally required to cope with the second. Our lives are marked by daily opportunities to define and summon physical, moral or psychological courage. When we call upon our courage, we grow our capacity to change the world around us and our lives.

Then things tend to go "back to normal."

Normal changes too. Sometimes drastically. For some of us, the event is a "game changer." It may be the result of suddenly losing a loved one, or the news of a terminal or life long illness, or the result of physical trauma that leaves you or someone close to you impaired for life. Life will never go back to normal.

Fortunately, normal is just a word. Unfortunately, these types of game changing events are inevitable regardless of our definition of normal. New normals call upon our Courage to Reflect, but it is the Courage to Adapt that carries us beyond—and back into living.

We all know of people who seem to be the recipients of really bad luck. It could be a friend with a severe heart condition wondering if today could be his last, or a relative who loses her husband in a freak accident at the prime of his life; it might be a family dealing with a child who will not experience growing up the way "normal" kids grow up.

These are but a few of the countless "There but by the grace of God, go I" scenarios we know all too well hold true. People for whom life will never be the same. People whose lives have never been "normal." How do they deal with this lot in life? After all, no one is immune to life's regular stressors and their challenges are that much greater. How do they do it?

We believe they survive, and in many cases thrive because they have found the Courage to Adapt. Human nature is a very complex and interesting thing. We have so many built-in mechanisms for interacting with our environment. Our greatest survival technique is the ability to adapt. That ability comes from being able to realize, or see reality for what it is. However, for many, getting to that point is a long and winding road with many gift shops along the way, none which seem to sell maps. That is why we wrote this book.

Beyond Fight, Flight or Entitlement

One of the greatest drawbacks we face in North American society is our past success and the false sense of security it fosters. Safe, healthy and living an arguably luxurious Western lifestyle, we have come to expect it might last forever. While recent economic events have served to illuminate the actual fragility of our society, true moral courage is required to understand the learning offered.

We genuinely believe that what we have is ours by right. After all, we have the receipts. We allow ourselves to believe that we are entitled to safety, happiness and health. When these things are challenged, we become very vocal, but rarely in the proactive sense. Instead, we moan, bitch and complain. We've all said *it*. Something along the lines of *"the government should do something about tha*t," or *"it's not my fault I'm in this situation so someone else should pay for this."*

We become moaning magnets, miring the like-minded in our lament or picking up the phone to invite friends and family to complain with us. Yet, nothing changes. Only when we find the Courage to Reflect and get back to engaging life proactively can we begin to make effective change. The Courage to Adapt our mindset allows us to experience life on a whole other wavelength.

OK, let's stop and think about change. Some degree of life's change is thrust upon us in those moments that define the act of living, particularly where game changers are concerned. Regardless, we all know of instances where life demands a reaction. These are the moments by which we define ourselves, courageously or otherwise.

As we mentioned earlier, our prehistoric brain presents us with two basic instincts: fight or flight. Fortunately, courage has taken us beyond such binary thinking. There are always three options: ignore it, a.k.a. hide or 'hope that it will go away'; counteract the imposed change to maintain "normal," or accept the change, adjust and move forward.

How does this relate to courage? Denying the reality of a significant challenge/fear/opportunity in our lives requires no courage. Implementing a counter change takes considerable courage and is often very effective. However, when the imposed change is both significant and permanent, the courage required to accept the change is often immense; herein, we must find the courage to accept and proactively re-engage life's new normal.

That new normal could mean coming to terms with living without someone who played a big part in our life or becoming responsible for the care and welfare of another. It might mean dealing with the fact that your life is not likely to be as long as you would like. New normals are global constants. We are sure you could come up with a long list of examples on your own.

"It's not having what you want, it's wanting what you've got," goes the line in a popular Sheryl Crow song. We could write a whole other book on the inspirational people we've come to know over the years who have found a way to summon the courage to thrive under unimaginable circumstances.

There Is No Going Back

The fact is that when some things change, the change is permanent. Ignoring it will only make things worse. There is no going back to the way it was, no compensation for what was lost, and no worth in complaining about it. The only rational thing to do is to accept the change for what it is: nothing bigger, nothing smaller. Then do what humans have been doing since the dawn of time—exercise your Courage to Adapt.

A BRIEF EXERCISE

Think of a game changing moment in your life. Write it down.

_____

_____

How did that moment impact your life?

_____

_____

_____

Write down three ways you have acted to adjust to your new normal.

1. _____

2. _____

3. _____

So, how do you evaluate the impact of such a permanent change? This is the point where you are going to need some courage.

Facing the inevitable can be a truly terrifying event for many. Taking stock of the impact of the change can be an exhausting and emotional task. However, if the task is approached practically, and emotions are controlled, the result can be liberating. Again, I refer to human nature. No matter how bad things are, they are rarely as bad as we think they are. Once we take stock of the impact, we can then truly see the change for what it is, not as we think it to be.

Then we can start to catalogue our options. What can we do? Who can help? Here's where finding the Courage to Adapt is rewarded. None of us are alone in life's journey. Open up to that realization and there is an abundance of help available from friends and strangers alike—as well as charitable organizations aligned with every game changer imaginable.

Finding the courage to seek and accept this help can be challenging for many. Yet, it exists and it exists because no matter what the change, there are those who have gone through much the same before you—and are now able, and quite willing, to help you do the same.

Once you have a list of options, you can start to build an action plan. This is commonly known as "playing the hand you're dealt" or making the best of what you have. Do not for a moment succumb to such thinking! Regardless of the hand you hold, if played with courage, it is a winning hand. Folding is not an option with the Courage to Adapt.

In the face of life's true challenges, instead of our mostly petty fears, we have the opportunity to grow and learn the most—the opportunity not only to survive, but to thrive as human beings. It is never easy; it is always worth it.

We don't all go seeking a brave new world. We all need the Courage to Adapt to the new worlds thrust upon us. When everything we take for granted changes, so must we all if we are to benefit from all Ten Steps to Courage. The final, the Courage to Adapt, is perhaps the steepest, but ultimately liberating—especially for those facing previously unimaginable game changers. We hope that you are never challenged to the 'nth' degree; if you are this tenth step is requisite for building a new courage for a new normal. We hope the skills outlined in this book can help you to make that transition and thrive.

As we have used the word, thrive, a few times in this chapter, let's define it in the greater context of courage. To flourish, prosper and succeed: we agree with the standard definition. We also think it important to point out that all of the above is possible in even the most demanding circumstances. You can flourish by becoming a stronger person than you ever thought possible. You can prosper by receiving intangible gifts of gratitude and support. You can succeed simply by surviving and accepting the fact that you have now become an inspiration for others.

The word thrive is relative. It all depends on what you value and how you express those values. What seems like the worst thing that could happen can bring out the best in you and others. If we can find the courage to see the best in others and ourselves, then no matter the circumstance—we thrive.

In the words of Stephen Hawking, the British physicist, *"Intelligence is the ability to adapt to change."* We are doing our best just to keep afloat in a world surfing on a sea of change. What are we willing to do about it? What can we do? Can we stop change? No. However, what we can do is adapt to a new reality. The Courage to Adapt is the key to a successful life in these times of accelerated change. What we adapt to is a life in which our reality is one of our own creation and re-creation.

The Courage to Adapt is one of the primary qualities of leadership and a life well-lived. It is the aspect of character that brings out the true leader within us all and carries us through the best and worst that comes our way.

Change is neither inherently good or bad—only our reaction to change might be judged as such. All kinds of conditions can change, some on a daily basis, some forever. From the weather to our welfare, we experience change as a constant. Without a doubt, the rate of ongoing change is greater now than at any other time in the history of the planet. We know that the world is changing with greater magnitude and velocity than we ever thought possible. The rate of change that we are experiencing is primarily driven by technological changes and is not the rate of human change. Moore's Law tells us that the number of transistors on integrated circuits doubles every two years. How much willingness do we as humans have to adapt to our new realities?

The question is, do we have the Courage to Adapt?

We find it helpful to reflect on the origin of the word adapt. It is from the Latin *"adaptare"* which means to *"fit."* To adapt to our new realities. To fit our new realities.

Fear is cheap. The Courage to Adapt is priceless.

Burn Your Business Plan, Embrace Your Principles

> "The key to good decision making is not knowledge. It is understanding. We are swimming in the former. We are desperately lacking in the latter."
>
> —Malcolm Gladwell

Lately, we have been challenging leaders to burn their business plans. We understand the attraction, but can anyone actually plan the future of a business? We might envision it. We might build action steps towards accomplishing particular goals. The trouble is no plan can render a business immune to change.

'What once worked does so no longer,' is a truth that some people and business have already taken to heart. Others have chosen to build better plans.

Rather than build a business plan, we encourage people to embrace a business model anchored by a single principle—the Courage to Adapt. With so many external agents of change acting upon the modern moment, such courage provides daily grounding and inspiration alike. Moreover it is a distinguishing characteristic of those individuals and businesses growing and succeeding in challenging times.

Another core characteristic is their willingness to embrace new models, to both adapt to new realities and positively co-create them. These outliers have harnessed the Courage to Adapt and with it changed their realities—and the world in which we live. They are the outliers of a courageous future for us all.

In taking the 10 Steps to Courageous Living to heart and practice you are an outlier; as such, we thank you in advance and encourage you to keep reading. Our steps might be drawing to a close, but not to an end.

The Courage to Adapt is thrust upon us all as individuals at various points in life. Our ability to rise above life's fears and challenges has brought us this far—in this book and our lives. Courage is always an individual choice.

On the other hand, the Courage to Adapt is not really a choice for any business seeking to thrive. It is an imperative. In this period of accelerated change, businesses need exactly this courage to leverage the opportunities that exist. Otherwise, for all the business plans crafted, everyone involved will have missed both the point and the opportunity entirely. A better mousetrap is not required if the mouse has left the house. More adaptable mindsets build better things.

The most effective way to change our mindset is to be proactive—in business as in life. By all means plot a course and set a pace, but always be prepared for the change to come. The alternative is akin to trying to outrun a tidal wave when change arrives.

We spend such a large percentage of our lives at work, it makes sense that courage be present there the most. Yet, as we know, the common work culture in North America does not thrive on such principle. Too rarely is it embodied or given voice by the principals. How then is it expected to flourish in the greater work culture? Bear in mind that innovation belongs to the courageous, not the always agreeable.

We think courage needs to become a bigger part of the business vocabulary and reside at the heart of all business cultures. It makes all things endurable, anything possible and opens the lines of true communication. Herein, innovation becomes less of an imperative and emerges as required—the always open resource of a company with the Courage to Adapt.

We know the difference it makes in our lives. We have similarly seen it put to work by some extraordinary people. We will introduce you to a few of them in the final part of this book. We all agree on at least one thing—courage can only take you to better places.

Change is happening. We have the benefit of that knowledge. Still, much of life is "business as usual". We cannot think of a more fitting metaphor for this change-resistance than dinosaur-like. In the midst of such change, we cannot afford to think as dinosaurs.

Science now seems to confirm the cause of dinosaurs' demise was meteoric, but as we know, there were survivors. What distinguished them? We think Charles Darwin had it right: *"It is not the strongest species that survive, nor the most intelligent, but the ones most responsive to change."* We with the Courage to Adapt.

15
Personal Action Plan

There you have it. Ten simple yet powerful steps that will provide you a clear path to a new and exciting life.

1. The Courage to Be

2. The Courage to Dream

3. The Courage to Trust

4. The Courage to Act

5. The Courage to Listen

6. The Courage to Tolerate

7. The Courage to Reflect

8. The Courage to Speak Up

9. The Courage to Say No

10. The Courage to Adapt

A BRIEF EXERCISE

Which of the above steps holds the greatest opportunity for you to strengthen the core courage of your life?

_____

If there were two things that you could do in the next seven days to help you get started, what would they be and when can you get started?

_____

_____

_____

What the kind of results would you expect to see?

_____

_____

_____

_____

_____

It IS as easy as that. Take a step and get out of the gate.

16
Emotional Hijacking

For much of his life, Ross was prone to emotional hijackings. Having come to understand what was really happening he created a strategy for effectively managing such events and has seen a huge improvement in his quality of life.

What is an emotional hijacking? Simply put, an emotional hijacking occurs when emotions explode before logical minds have an opportunity to catch up and filter automatic—and all too often regrettable—responses. In the case of an emotional hijacking, when our buttons are pushed our reaction is both automatic and entirely fear-based.

With the Courage to Listen, Reflect and Adapt, the hijacker becomes nothing more than a "Hi, Jack, er . . . in your opinion." While it is said we are judged by our actions, it is our reactions that can prove most costly.

Without doubt, these emotional hijackings can be very expensive, especially where the other parties involved are concerned. For those unfamiliar with the techniques for handling such a moment, the emotional hijacking can spread as an over-reactive contagion. Chain reactions are not uncommon and can only serve to perpetuate conflict. Most costly are the ruptures in relationships that can endure for years or a lifetime.

So, with the 10 Steps to Courageous Living in mind, we can agree on two things: emotional hijackings are something we all need to avoid and that we ourselves are the primary source of the emotional hijacking—regardless of external antagonism.

In the absence of a developed sense of self and personal courage, emotional hijackings are almost inevitable. It is perhaps because such behavior has become fairly common in North American society, that we seem to always be waving the finger of fear in the face of our 'opponents' and selves alike.

Without exploring the deeper definitions of courage, as we have now done together, we leave ourselves open to all fears, both real and imagined, that modern life has to offer. An openness to all that life has to offer need only extend as far as it fills and inspires your life. Remember, we have our filters, and our moral and psychological courage, to keep us sane and sound.

Without those fundaments, we are left open to effects of fear. Before long, we can become it. It is through that opening that the emotional hijacker is allowed to explode those fears—using our own fear-driven words or actions as incendiary.

What is the fear that ignites emotional hijackings? As explored earlier, if you give in to fear you will find reason to fear plenty of things.

In our line of work and by virtue of our vocation we bring out the emotional hijacker in others. In the last little while, we have survived a trio of emotional hijackers on our doorstep. As always, we were ready for the explosive outbursts of their respective fears: being excluded, failure and conflict.

Had we allowed ourselves to return salvo and defend, the scenarios would not have each ended so amiably. By recognizing their fear, listening to them and by refusing to react in a retaliatory fashion, we are pleased to report we were able in each case to save the relationship in question.

Put Pavlov's Pooch to Rest

Stephen Covey tells us that what separates us from the rest of the animal kingdom is the freedom to choose what lies between stimulus and response. It is our ability to access that nanosecond or two of courage that allows us to respond accordingly with consideration and a rational mind rather than react with emotionally hijacked reflexes.

If your auto-pilot is set for emotional hijacking, or if you live or work with emotional hijackers in your midst, let this book be your reminder. Our ability to respond rather than react is an innate gift that we can all further develop. It enables us to leave our less and automatic selves behind and embrace a new possibility for engaging life's ongoing challenges.

If you simply acknowledge that this freedom to choose is half of the solution, you step beyond emotional hijackings and help others do the same. The remainder revolves around not allowing ourselves to get caught in the cycle of destruction. We are amazed what can be achieved in a nanosecond or two in terms of creating more consistently positive outcomes.

We don't have to be Pavlov's dogs, do we? We can do so much better.

By not allowing yourself to be hijacked by a fear based emotional-reaction and by recognizing the fear based emotional reactions you see in others, you will enhance the quality of your life and of others.

One of the best antidotes we have found for bringing down an emotional hijacker in our presence is the most simple. We listen without defensive reproach—either in our body or on our lips. This allows us to listen carefully. We hear the fear. When the opening presents itself we offer something like, "Bob, I wonder if you could show me a little latitude on this. I would sure appreciate it. Do you think you could help me out?"

It is amazing how these simple words help to bring people from the fear-based, attack mode to a place where they are open and receptive to working with you to explore the possibilities.

Remember that all emotional hijackings are fear-based reactions, albeit with very different origin stories. People feel threatened. In the grip of fear, emotionally they are ready to go to war.

When you experience an emotional hijacking within yourself the most effective strategy is clear. Do not react. Access the Freedom to Choose and choose to respond rather than react. Even at this point, the emotions can still be running pretty high. Rather than risk a late rush of adrenalized response, buy time with body language which speaks your understanding and intent.

Allow your own automatic response systems to calm and listen. As they talk your adrenalin will come down. Interestingly, so will their own levels of adrenalin decrease, whether through sheer emotional expenditure or sympathetic influence. Remember, courage can be as contagious as fear—as can the calm it encourages.

Moreover, what they have to say may be different than what you thought they meant.

17
The Four Fatal Fears

Our basic conditioning was written over 100,000 generations ago, a distant past during which fear was crucial to survival. Roaming the plains, honing our legacy of hunter-gatherer instincts, fear was a very real constant companion and survival a daily endeavor. Survival required our full attention and a long life was extremely uncommon.

Much has changed since. Survival rates are certainly higher. We no longer need be concerned with saber-toothed tigers. Big picture? We live in a world where we no longer are as likely to be harmed. Nonetheless, the fundamental fears and the automatic response systems they can trigger, still exist.

Without doubt, and for better and worse, our society and technologies have evolved. The same cannot be said of our most primitive fears. However, with courage we can evolve a far more positive response system to the fears that we face each and every day.

We may be wearing a nice golf shirt with khakis and sitting behind the wheel of the family SUV on the way to our comfortable homes with all of the benefits of a security system, power, heat and running water—yet to a large degree we are hard wired by our prehistoric fears. These fears that were key to survival millions of years ago are now our greatest weakness.

The four fatal fears that we see most people suffer from are . . .

1. I need to succeed. (Fear of Failure)

2. I need to be right. (Fear of Being Wrong)

3. I need to be needed. (Fear of Rejection)

4. I need to be comfortable. (Fear of Discomfort)

You will notice that we led with the need rather than the fear. Isn't that typically how we hear it? People often express their needs, yet seldom come clean about their fears. Our needs fuel our fears. In turn, our fears are the true source of what we express as our needs. It takes courage to put our fears first in our mind's eye and we have done that together throughout this book.

Now conscious of courage on multiple levels, let's take a closer look at each of the four fatal fears.

Fear of Failure

If there is one thought that pervades modern society it is that winning is everything and losing is to be avoided—at all cost. We would argue that cost has been too high for society and individual alike. The unfortunate result of this misplaced thinking is that people simply stop trying. They no longer take risks. They avoid win or lose scenarios and end up playing it safe. Rather than winding up safe, they live their life playing not to lose.

Isn't that sad? Ross will often challenge people with a question about what they fear. He often hears that they don't fear anything. Upon closer questioning, the reason for that 'zero' fear attitude is that they don't risk putting themselves in situations where there is something to fear. Not only are they playing not to lose, they seldom "show up" even when present.

Fear of Being Wrong

The second fatal fear that we often see, particularly among the more technically-inclined, is the fear of being wrong. When lives and careers are built around what we know, rarely do we make time for what others think. The funny thing about this is that in this case, we might never know even a fraction of what there is to be known.

Fear fatalists of every variety seek to protect themselves. They ensure that remaining on the edge of life's happenings where their intelligence might not truly be tested— nor contribute. They will never risk being wrong and they will certainly never admit to a mistake. Their fear keeps them stuck where they are. Their minds remain closed to the possibility of learning from others. All too often, their need to be right pushes others out of their lives. They would rather de-people their lives than admit to being wrong about anything.

Fear of Rejection

The third fatal fear is another we all know well. It is the fear of rejection which comes from our need to be accepted. What do we do? Fearing rejection, we are really good at avoiding situations where we might risk not being accepted. Our fear tells us that it is better to hide in the hills and become a hermit than face the fear of possibly being rejected. This fear of rejection is often seen in a work environment where people choose not to "show up" with their thoughts. People who fear being rejected will not speak up. This fatal flaw is especially dangerous if it is present in a corporate culture because this is where groupthink finds its origins.

Fear of Discomfort

The fourth fatal fear is most specifically about being emotionally uncomfortable. We get all kinds of weird looks when we talk about the need to get comfortable being uncomfortable. *"Oh, I don't feel comfortable doing that."* We hear this all of the time—especially when we are asking people to stretch and do things for the first time.

So many of our physical discomforts are catered to in modern society, we forget that life's greater opportunities requires us to reach beyond our comfort zone. Most often, what we are asking of them is to be more proactive and courageous than they have been in the past. Are you going to die from the discomfort that ensues? Probably not.

People who work to shelter themselves from being emotionally uncomfortable are the ones that will never make a presentation to a group. They will never make a sales call. They will never reach out and ask for help. They will never explore new territory or try new things because they are afraid of looking foolish and they tell themselves that they will be "embarrassed to death." Wow, it amazes us how much power we give our fears!

If you aren't comfortable being uncomfortable then we can guarantee you that you will never learn like others because learners are always trying new things, making mistakes and bouncing back. Once people understand what we mean about getting comfortable with discomfort, they see the opportunity to grow. They know that they have lived a sheltered life. They have lived their lives with all kinds of anxieties that keep them from asking for help, looking foolish or appearing vulnerable. At the same time, the Fear of Discomfort has cheated them from really living their lives.

If you are entirely comfortable doing what you are doing, you better give your head a shake—odds are good you are cheating yourself.

18
Stepping Beyond the Four Fatal Fears

We think the 10 Steps to Courageous Living offers a great path to the peaks of your potential. Consider the Four Fatal Fears nothing more than the moguls and obstacles that define the other side of the mountain.

Here is where a ski analogy brings the latter into perspective. If you are on a ski hill and running flat on your skis, chances are you are probably feeling pretty comfortable. Anyone who has skied realizes that the real thrill from the sport comes when you are up on your edges. With the boundaries already set on the hill, the only other limits are in your approach to the mountain. On the far side of being up on your edges lies true growth.

Let's stop looking elsewhere for the courage to change. Let's stretch our minds and hearts to carry that courage beyond this book and into our lives. Then, let's each stake a commitment to step out of the gate and prepare to be amazed at a world in which fear is not the overriding principle.

It is said that each day we make approximately a dozen key choices. The choice is ours to make in every instance. When we make the same choice repeatedly, it becomes part of our way of being. In time, it becomes our life.

When we consistently allow fear to guide our choices, our opportunities for courage and growth diminish accordingly. Herein, a life of fear becomes not only delimited, but punishing. Guided by our most primitive instincts, we can make very bad choices that will impact more than our lives alone.

Rather than suffering the indignity of our most pre-historic fears for even one day longer, we need to exercise our Freedom to Choose. We need to exercise our courage of conscious choice to gain control of the auto-pilot and disarm the emotional hijacker, both within and in others.

What we need most are more models of courage in our midst. We mentioned knowing more than few of those outliers earlier.

19
Courage, Encourage & Discourage

The English language is fascinating. We find it fascinating because we often take one word and turn it in to several words to extend the original meaning or to describe the various impacts of the original word. The word "courage" is an excellent example to which we have paid no small attention in this book.

However, we have yet to talk about how courage can be influenced. How courage can be "encouraged" by others, or how courage can be "discouraged" by others. On the whole, we tend to use these words without much thought about their power—or their influence on the actions of others and ourselves.

Earlier, we discussed courage as coming from within. As much a mindset as a muscle, courage stems from the development of your internal thought processes. The decision to do something courageous can only be made by the person executing the courageous act.

We don't say things like *"I will encourage myself to do that"* or *"I discouraged myself from doing that."* Encouragement and discouragement are external. For example *"I strongly encouraged my son to try again after falling off his bike." "I did everything I could to discourage her from quitting her job over that silly argument."* The interesting thing is that it often takes an act of courage to either encourage or discourage another; it might even foster an act of courage in return. Peer pressure works both ways. Let your courage be the guiding force.

Peer pressure is something we have all felt in our life at some time or another. Whether subtle or obvious, peer pressure is always grounded in encouragement or discouragement. Its power comes from the collective belief that if everyone else is doing something, you have the permission and encouragement of the group to do the same. The opposite also applies. So when you show up to a party wearing last year's style, you are targeted. The perceived pressure to conform can be tremendous.

This is amplified by the fact that when we are children, we are taught that we need external permission for practically everything. Yet, when we become adults, we are suddenly expected to think for ourselves. The permission we need can only come from within.

We should know what's right and wrong for us. We should know how to govern ourselves when it comes to eating, drinking, working, playing and so on. For some, the transition is natural. For others, the transition into adulthood is difficult, and leaves us susceptible to the influence of others. Our sense of self is immature, and as a result we look to others to give us permission in life. The reality is that we are not making independent mature decisions, but following perceived cues in order to "fit in".

As human beings, we are essentially tribal. We all feel the need to fit in. While there are a few notable exceptions to this, as a species we need to feel a sense of belonging. That's what keeps us social and gives us the ability to work together. Yet, somehow, we also feel the need to be individuals who need to express ourselves. We need to be heard. We need to know that what we think is important. How do we reconcile this dilemma?

Whether we are aware of it or not, we tend to gravitate to other people who are like-minded. People who share enough common thought processes that we can get along with them without too much friction. This way, we are tolerated when we express ourselves and develop a bond because we can relate to how others within the group see the world. This all works nicely until you have a point of view that doesn't quite fit with the "tribe."

Like everyone else, you have a need to be heard and communicate your thoughts. Moreover, you likely have questions. When you summon the Courage to Speak Up, you invariably find many people willing to offer advice. As much encouragement and discouragement you might receive, do not confuse it for anything other than advice alone. For those with a fear of speaking up, to discover the world is full of people willing to share their advice can be a tremendous realization.

Just remember, everyone has an opinion. Giving advice is specifically so easy because it is essentially effortless. The effort and actions to be taken thereafter are yours alone. Again, the action must be taken by you. This is why we almost always seek advice from people we know share our sense of values and have similar moral codes.

While encouragement and discouragement may influence your sense of courage, neither can bring you true courage. And remember, advice comes with no strings attached. The degree of courage required is always measured by the level of consequence. Deep down we know this, yet our society suffers a courage deficit while advice comes cheap. Regardless of encouragement or discouragement of others, the Freedom to Choose and what you choose is your responsibility alone. Recognizing that takes true courage, especially when factoring the predominance and vested interest of so many in our lives. Beyond personal relationships we see this in the advertising we are bombarded with.

Advertisements seek to influence us on every level daily and works the twin paddles of encouragement and discouragement expertly. *Stop using A. Trust B. Don't be C. Be D. Buy E or F will happen. Buy G if you care about family. Save big. Save yourself. Be more. Buy now.* However, for all the encouragement and discouragement offered by the advertising in our lives, the sum of what it amounts to is simple—buy more.

Obeying other signs in life, road signs in particular, could save your life. Just as surely, disobeying them could result in losing your life or your taking the life of another. Yet, all a road sign can really do is either encourage you or discourage you to take action. The Freedom to Choose is always yours.

Why is any of this relevant to you being courageous? Well, it's important to understand the responsibility we take on when we encourage or discourage others. We generally engage in this activity by dispensing advice. Younger people are known to use this tool to encourage people to do things they themselves would not do in order to be entertained. On the surface, this all looks quite innocent. In reality these people are practicing the art of persuasion. As with any art, it has its dark side. Unfortunately, it is one that has been encouraged for much of the last century of business culture—and pretty much all of human history.

The point to be made here is that when we encourage or discourage someone, we have to know when advice becomes persuasion. While persuasion in some cases is very appropriate, it is also very easy to abuse. Persuasion is defined by Encyclopedia Britannica as *"the process by which a person's attitudes or behavior are, without duress, influenced by communications from other people."*

We have the duty to determine whether our intent is to offer advice to help someone make up their mind or to turn their minds to our own intent. It is equally important for the person seeking advice to understand the difference and govern themselves by similar principle. Neither encouragement nor discouragement should be given or taken lightly.

On the broadest levels of influence, society as we know it has used encouragement and discouragement to maintain order, control societal norms and transfer wisdom. On a face to face level, persuasion has become a common technique used by people with both personal and professional agendas to have others do their bidding.

At work, we are faced with both solicited and unsolicited encouraging/discouraging forces all the time. These external forces at times have agendas attached that are not always in your best interest. Wading through all this information can be a daunting task, to discern what your opinion should be distracts you from the entire point of having an opinion to offer.

Remember, only you can take action and only you will be held responsible and accountable for that action. That's why it is important to recognize that you get to decide what encouragement or discouragement you seek. You get to decide whether or not it will influence your action. You are not obligated to take any action as a result, but you just might surprise yourself.

Ironically, we are about to encourage you to evaluate the impact or consequences of any action before you adopt advice from anyone—including us. Moreover, we discourage following the influence of any source of encouragement or discouragement that you cannot identify as trustworthy. At times, it pays to play it safe. Better advice always awaits from those with your best interests at heart.

20
Responsibility

What kind of environment needs to exist for courage to prosper? As humans we tend to want to take the path of least resistance. It's easier to let someone else deal with things that are potentially controversial or confrontational. As long as we don't take on the responsibility, we don't wear the bulls-eye. We don't have to be courageous.

The truth is both simple and sad. If we don't take on the responsibility, we can't be courageous. It's simply impossible!

The opposite is also true. Once you have taken responsibility for something, if required, you have no choice but to be courageous! So, it makes sense that courage comes from a sense of responsibility. It is internal, not external.

Many people think that they hold people responsible by virtue of their command and titles alone. We've all heard it before. *"Joe, I'm going to make you responsible for this project." "Jane, I'm giving you the responsibility to make sure everyone attends the meeting."* When we hear those kinds of statement, we laugh! You can't give someone the responsibility for anything! People need to "take" the responsibility! You can ask someone if they are willing to take on a responsibility, but make no mistake, you cannot "give" someone responsibility—you can only offer the opportunity.

Will you be successful? Will your courage result in the desired outcome? Who knows? What we do know is that without assuming responsibility in your life and for your life, you will absolutely and unfortunately fail to be courageous.

Can you share responsibility? No! Responsibility is absolute!

You are either responsible or you're not. You may be responsible for a section of a project, but for that segment, you are totally responsible. No one else. If courage is required to complete your responsibility, then you are compelled to act courageously. If you do not, you have effectively given up your sense of responsibility.

If you have truly accepted your responsibility then you will do whatever it takes. Each of the 10 Steps to Courageous Living leads someplace better. Collectively, they guide you within and bring cause and consideration to your dreams and actions.

What courage offers is a better life that works wonders in the lives of everyone around you. At work as in life—take courage to heart, make its wisdom your art. In return, it will lead you places beyond your imagination.

21
Models of Courage

As we continue to work with others seeking to strengthen their courage, we have learned to look well beyond ourselves for inspiration. We find a lot of people coming to us without a good role model for real courage in life.

Fortunately, for over 30 years we have been honoured to work with some very courageous people—people who are as courageous in business as they are in all aspects of their lives.

Without digging into the common historical archive, we would like to introduce you to some of the people we consider our Models of Courage today.

Emmie Leung

One of the most courageous leaders we have ever worked with is Emmie Leung. Emmie is both the founder and CEO of the Emterra Group of Companies and has been a pioneer in the recycling and waste diversion industry for 35 years. If there is one thing that all pioneers need it is courage. From her start as a one-person operation, she has grown Emterra into an international organization with 800 employees and annual revenues in excess of $100 million.

As a young woman growing up in Hong Kong during the 1960s, Emmie realized early that if she wanted to escape a traditional, subservient role, she needed to move to North America; once there, she could pursue the business education she hungered for and find opportunities that she would not be afforded in Hong Kong. From very humble beginnings as an impoverished student immigrating to

Winnipeg in the 1970s, Emmie graduated from the University of Manitoba with a degree in Commerce—exactly as she had desired. With a meager thousand dollar savings to get started at school, she financed her way through university, waitressing at restaurants in Winnipeg. She came to love Canada and upon graduation wanted to remain. However, as a young Asian woman, with less than perfect English, she was unable to secure a job.

After months of searching, Emmie decided to create her own job and started her one person business in Vancouver, operating out of a basement apartment with an old rundown van. She started distributing flyers door-to-door in the affluent Point Grey area of Vancouver, letting folks know that she would be back to collect their old papers and cardboard. She did it all. She printed and distributed the flyers, drove the van and collected the discarded paper and cardboard. The latter she stored in her apartment and when she had collected enough she hand-loaded it into a container for shipment to Asia.

You see, Emmie was the CEO of her very own one person company, International Paper Industries. However, she was also the driver, forklift operator, shipper and accountant. Are you starting to see why we call Emmie not only one of the most courageous, but also one of the most committed people we know? From the start, she had courage to get started and the commitment to keep going.

Today, Emmie has created a network of recycling facilities across Canada and in the US and the Emterra Group of Companies consists of three divisions: Emterra Environmental, Emterra Tire Recycling and Canadian Liquids Processing Ltd.

Emterra Environmental serves more than 80 Canadian

municipalities and markets half a million tons of recyclable products per year; fully 70 per cent of those recyclables are reused in North America. From a one person business built because nobody would hire her, Emmie has created one of the largest, privately-held, integrated-resource management companies in Canada.

We can all learn so much from her story alone. So much of what Emmie has achieved, she has done so on her own, especially in the early years.

So if Emmie can achieve what she did as an impoverished immigrant to Canada who nobody would hire even after she graduated from university, what is holding us back? We need to meet more models of courage in our life and courage is the one quality that Emmie embodies most.

As Emmie explained, *"it is not just the courage to get started, but the commitment to keep going when one encounters the speed bumps on the road of life."* That is what has made the difference in her life.

Emmie values her courage. It provided her with exactly what she wanted—to create her own life on her own terms. It took Courage for her to come to Canada. The Courage to dream and the Courage to Act led to the creation of her own business.

Our experience has been that if you put those two Courages together you have a powerful formula for success.

Did Emmie always envision what it could be? Of course not. However, what she did see were the next logical steps. Once she gained clarity on the actions required, Emmie took action. The results have been positive.

We are reminded of the Joel Barker quote: *"Vision without Action is just a dream. Action without Vision just passes the time. Vision with Action can change the world."* Not only has Emmie changed her own world, she has taken responsibility for it. Each day, she goes to work to make the world a better place—one that minimizes harmful legacies of landfill and incineration and strives to meet maximum recycling potential.

Every day she changes the world for the better: for the 800 employees of her company, the hundreds of thousands of people her company services across Canada and the millions more dependent on Emmie and Emterra to provide that better world.

Where others are drowning in bureaucracy, Emmie leaves others choking in her dust. She is a woman of action with a clear vision.

Emmie understands the Law of Forward Motion and has helped countless others play it forward. Recently in Winnipeg, a city that is very futuristic when it comes to considering environmental responsibilities, Emmie gave wheels to their vision of a cleaner fleet of waste service trucks. To reduce the greenhouse gas producing carbons of the traditional diesel fueled garbage trucks generate, the City of Winnipeg switched to a fleet of trucks utilizing natural gas. Emmie is the one who made it happen.

Winnipeg is now home to the largest cold weather fleet of natural gas-powered trucks in the world—thanks to Emmie's courage to step up and make this dream a reality.

Emmie also possesses the Courage to Listen. She does this everyday—by walking around her operations and practicing the Courage to Listen to others. If there is one thing that Emmie is not it is a remote CEO parked atop an ivory tower.

What does this do for her? We suspect that very few CEOs of an international organization have anywhere near the frontline, day-to-day understanding of what is really happening in their businesses the way that Emmie does.

Can a leader be both compassionate and courageous? Absolutely. At a time when so many leaders have lost touch with their people Emmie is at the other end of the spectrum, connecting with her people in a caring way.

Emmie has come a long way from her days of working as a waitress in Winnipeg for $1.40 an hour. Emmie often lived on Cheese Whiz and rice saving her last 20 dollars for a bus pass to get to university. Nonetheless, for all her success since, Emmie continues to lead a simple life.

Now, as Emmie's daughters Paulina and Vivian become more and more involved in the leadership of Emterra, we see the same courageous qualities in them that Emmie has modeled to them all of their lives.

Dreams alone can be converted to reality through planning and action. Fantasies are not only foolish, but fear-based as well. Which is why to dream effectively, as Emmie does daily, makes courage come to life.

Consider what Emmie achieved as a result of acting on her dream. If one thing can be said about Emmie and the members of her National Leadership Team it is this—if they say they are going to do something, they do it. Done or certain to soon be so. Sure, sometimes life surprises them at work too and action lists shift. Their priorities do not and they always successfully execute, especially when things don't work according to plan.

Emmie Leung knows the value of plans well enough, but

it is her courage and commitment that has carried her over life's speed bumps large and small. Emmie is a model of courage.

Ted Kuntz

Let us tell you about our friend Ted Kuntz. Ted is a gifted psychotherapist in private practice in Vancouver, Canada. He is also the author of an incredible book, *Peace Begins With Me*, that teaches people how to live life peacefully and joyfully.

Ted and Ross have also co-facilitated many workshops and presentations together. What Ross admires most about Ted is his ability to see through the confusion and identify core truths. Ted's most valuable skill though is his courage to speak up and tell his truth.

Ted communicates his truth clearly, compassionately and respectfully. His compassion comes from a genuine belief that we are all doing the best we can with what we know. He also recognizes that our best may not be good enough. He combines his deep caring for others with the ability to guide people to make changes in their lives.

Ted's journey has not been easy. His father died when Ted was five years old leaving his mother a widow with six children. As a result, Ted learned to take responsibility for his life at an early age.

Later in life, his journey was impacted again, this time by his son Joshua. Joshua became disabled at five months of age due to the unintended effects of a childhood vaccine. Ted credits Josh with being his greatest teacher in life.

Ted learned to confront truth on this journey and learned the value of truth-telling. Ted often shares the story of when the chief neurologist at the local children's hospital told him not to bring his son back to the hospital; he admitted they couldn't improve his son's medical condition. This rare example of truth telling helped Ted make peace with his son's condition.

While working with Ted to co-facilitate leadership development workshops and strategic planning sessions, Ross learned many things. At the top of the list of things he has come to value most in Ted is his Courage to Speak Up.

Here is a brief interview we conducted with our friend Ted on the Courage to Speak Up.

Ted, have you always possessed the Courage to Speak Up or how did it evolve for you?

I didn't always have the courage to speak up. As a matter of fact I was shy and introverted. My shyness (and lack of courage) almost cost me my first job in my chosen profession. I was hired to be a child care counselor with a residential treatment facility in Vancouver (Coquitlam) for teenagers with behavioral challenges. The nature of the clientele meant the work was demanding and constantly shifting to respond to the diverse needs of the youths admitted into the program.

Each week a staff meeting was held to review the week's activities and brainstorm ideas as to how we might best serve the needs of these struggling and acting-out youth. My supervisor expected each of us to offer our ideas and insights. I was too nervous to risk sharing the many ideas swimming through my mind. Each time it was my turn to speak, I found a way to decline. I'd say things like—*"I'm still finding my way around here"* and *"I'm still formulating my thoughts."* One meeting after I had once again avoided risking my ideas my supervisor said, *"Ted, that's the last time you get to bow out of the conversation. The next time I hear an excuse as to why you can't contribute, you're fired."*

I was shocked by the suddenness and firmness of my supervisor's statement. *"Am I not doing good work?"* I asked. *"You're doing great work. And that's why I need your ideas. But if you are not willing to share them then you are not much good to us,"* she responded. This supervisor gave me a tremendous gift. She recognized I had something valuable to offer and insisted that I take a risk and share my ideas with others. I have never forgotten that lesson.

And now you have passed that on to others including myself. Congratulations. Ted what do you think gets in the way of people Speaking Up?

In my work with clients, both at the individual and family level, as well as the organizational and community level, I've learned that life is complex. For much of our history as an organized society, we have lived with a hierarchical form of leadership. This is where a few people at the top make decisions for those lower in the hierarchy. This model of leadership may have served us well in past civilizations. It no longer works today. Life is too complex and complicated to rely on the wisdom and perspective of a few individuals. We need the collective wisdom of all of us to solve our challenges.

Nature shows us the value of collective wisdom. A hive of bees, a school of fish, a flock of birds is fifty times more responsive to its environment than any individual bee, fish or bird. The same is true for us. Collectively we hold more wisdom than any one individual. This wisdom is only valuable though if it's shared, and unfortunately few people have the courage to speak up and share their wisdom.

That is so true. Without the synergy that comes from what you call the collective wisdom, we are left primarily with our thoughts alone. As you work with people in your practice, what do you see as the main reasons for their lack of courage?

I believe there are a number of reasons for this dearth of courage. One is we have been socialized for centuries to follow the direction of our leaders whether it is our parents, elders, teachers or bosses. Compliance has been rewarded.

Robert Kiyosaki, author of *Rich Dad, Poor Dad*, declares that our education system has been intentionally designed to create employees. People who show up on time, follow direction, and go home on time. Kiyosaki's argument is that if you want to be wealthy you need to learn how to evaluate risk and make your own decisions. Few of us have been taught to evaluate risk and make our own decisions.

There is also a lack of real leadership in our society. Most leaders want good followers. This might keep the leader in a leadership position, but doesn't provide real leadership. I subscribe to the definition of leadership that says a great leader is one who develops the leadership of others. But this kind of leadership takes courage too. Many leaders are fearful that their subordinates will surpass them and thus they do whatever they can to keep their colleagues small.

We will not succeed if we keep people small and silent. Hewlett Packard, the internationally successful computer manufacturer, recognized the value their employees make to their success. They also understood that the computer industry changes very quickly, and that in order to remain successful and profitable they needed to keep changing and reinventing themselves. In short, they needed all the good ideas they could find. In an effort to stimulate employee ideas and the courage to act on their ideas HP created Ten Commandments for Employees. Two of my favorites are: 1. Come to work each day willing to be fired. 2. It's easier to ask for forgiveness than for permission.

I witness an absence of courage in both the corporate world and the political world. Two of our most powerful institutions for creating change are handcuffed by a lack of willingness of its constituents to speak up and challenge the status quo. A friend of mine who is an elected official with a local government confided that he has no power to make decisions. Most all decisions, he said, are made by a handful of people. The rest of us are simply expected to support those decisions whether we agree with them or not.

I know exactly what you mean. There seems to be a shift towards a totalitarian style of leadership in business and politics. One of the areas that we get pushback from leaders on is letting go and allowing people to make what might be called mistakes. Why is it so challenging to convince people these mistakes can actually lead to very good things?

One of the areas where I witness the greatest absence of courage is the courage to make mistakes. Not only to risk making a mistake, but the willingness to admit when one's actions/decisions are not working. The fact is every policy, strategy, and action is an experiment. We don't know with certainty the outcome of our decisions no matter how well researched or conceived. History is replete with examples of decisions that produced drastic unintended outcome—thalidomide, residential schools, vaccines, DDT, GMOs, etc. If we are unable to admit that our actions are experiments and treat them as experiments, we will never properly collect and evaluate the data to determine whether our actions were the right actions.

I understand why people are afraid to make mistakes. We are often punished for our mistakes. Society tends to focus more on justice than on learning. Rather than investing our energy in discovering what we can learn from a 'mistake', we direct our attention at passing judgment and exacting justice. Consequently it takes courage to admit one has made a mistake, but until we step into our courage and tell the truth we are trapped in actions and strategies that are simply ineffective.

We like what you say about the Courage to Speak Up really being about the courage to tell the truth. Could you talk a little more about that for us?

I witness a lack of courage to speak up and tell the truth at every level of organization, from the largest corporations to our most intimate relationships. Much of my work is with couples struggling in their marriage. The most common reason for failed marriages is a failure to communicate. And what is not being communicated is truth.

I consistently witness couples concealing their truth rather than revealing their truth. I believe this broad and pervasive failure is the result of the agreement most couples make when they come together in marriage. Most couples make a commitment to "love each other 'til death do us part."

In my experience, this agreement, this vow, causes individuals to withhold any truth that may challenge their commitment to be together. If something emerges that may potentially threaten the relationship, rather than put it out on the table and address it directly, it remains hidden and concealed. It is this concealing that ultimately causes most relationships to fail. It is also what causes most businesses to fail. In their need to be right most leaders fail to invite discussion about what isn't working.

I believe a better agreement for two people to enter into is the agreement to 'tell the truth.' In my experience, truth telling is the core foundation of a long and successful relationship. Those relationships that are successful, and business is simply an extended relationship, are ones where people reveal truth rather than conceal truth. Some of my greatest heroes in the world today are 'whistleblowers': those who have the courage to stand up and declare that something is wrong even if it may cost them their employment and sometimes their life.

I believe our failure to tell our truth is the result of having an inappropriate sense of responsibility. Most people withhold truth because of concern as to how others will respond to their telling the truth. I've learned that I am not responsible for another's response. I am only responsible for telling my truth. I am responsible for sharing my perspective as clearly and as respectfully as possible. How another chooses to respond is their responsibility.

Final words of wisdom?

Most of us are overly sensitive to how others might respond. In being overly sensitive we give away our power to tell our truth. As I was learning to tell my truth and to take responsibility for me rather than others, I carried a simple reminder in my wallet—"What others think about me is none of my business."

Ted Kuntz is a model of courage.

Andrew Kemp

Andrew Kemp is another strong model of courage in our lives. He is CEO of the regional insurance brokerage firm CMW Insurance and growing happier every day. Eight years ago, Andrew left the bureaucracy of international corporate life behind. He hasn't looked back and for good reason. He is happy.

Much of the success that he enjoys and allows others to enjoy boils down to courage.

Andrew attended the University of British Columbia where he graduated with a degree in Economics and joined a large international insurance brokerage firm the day after finishing his final exams. Later on in his 19 year career with his first employer Andrew says, "*I realized that a large company just wasn't conducive to the best things for our clients or for the employees.*"

In 2004, frustrated with the bureaucracy of a large international corporation, Andrew joined CMW Insurance and within eight years has the regional firm well on their way to the magic $100 million mark. With Andrew's courageous leadership at the helm, CMW has earned a reputation for being one of the fastest-growing commercial insurance brokerage firms in the industry.

Andrew was only 24 years old when his mother, who was in her fifties, died and he knew that she left her life with many intentions left unfulfilled. Andrew's mother had always been a model of drive and determination for him. Seeing her life cut short at an early age left him committed to living courageously and in the moment. Andrew promised himself to live life now—with a focus on enjoying the journey, not just the destination.

When we listen to Andrew's story we are reminded of many aspects of courage in his life. After a 19 year career with a global corporation he had the Courage to Reflect on his life. He came to the realization that if he didn't change something that it wouldn't be long before he became an unhappy, disgruntled, heart attack candidate. Despite the fact that he was seen as a rising star in the organization, he found the Courage to let go of what he had known. He found the courage to see a different way of being himself—but happier. The Courage to Act came naturally.

That said, of all of the courages that Andrew embodies, the one that we admire most is his willingness to have the courage to say "no." We see so many leaders distracted by the wrong things. Andrew clearly knows what the right thing is and that is what allows him to say no to the wrong things . . . the noise and the mud that clutter our minds and litter our desks.

As the CEO of a successful and growing firm it is easy to get sucked into the thick of thin things. Yet Andrew consistently keeps one thing—the client—at the top of his list and works hard to avoid being dragged into issues that are less important. His attitude and approach have served as both a benchmark and a beacon. As he models that behavior it sends a powerful message to all of his team about what really matters at CMW.

We believe that life is about choices and that there always is a choice. Andrew sees things a little differently. His take on it is that he often really doesn't have a choice when it comes to leadership. What needs be done, must be done for the betterment of everyone involved. As CEO, Andrew holds himself responsible to everyone in the organization. He is responsible for the health and wealth of the workplace and if that is being threatened it is his responsibility to address it.

Compare this to other organizations where the tendency is to abdicate responsibility to someone else. People issues are definitely not the domain of HR and middle management alone. Leadership needs to be encouraged throughout and embodied at the top as it is at CMW.

Knowing Andrew the way that we do it will be interesting to see where courage takes him—moving forward with the customer top of mind is the only certainty.

Andrew Kemp is a model of Courage.

Dann Konkin

Our final model of courage will inspire anyone with a dream. Dann Konkin is the first to acknowledge he is a dreamer. In public school, more than one teacher told his parents that Dann had to stop daydreaming in class. Dann did not and even those teachers can likely admire where Dan's daydreams have led.

Dann is the CEO of Ampco Manufacturers Inc, the family firm that he joined in 1976 after completing his education and traveling in Europe and Africa. His teachers never dreamt his daydreams would dare lead so far. For the 100 people that work at Ampco, their families and the firm's clients, the good news is that Dann has never stopped dreaming. That is exactly why he succeeds the way that he does.

It was the Courage to Dream that has enabled Dann to build the family business from half a million dollars of annual revenue to approaching twenty million of annual revenue in the years that he has led the firm.

Consistently, we see Dann accessing the Courage to Dream as he continues to shape the future of Ampco.

Dann says it best in his own words: "If I am not doing it, who is? I cannot ever remember not dreaming about things in my life. When I was young, I always dreamt of things that I wanted in life. I knew I wanted to live in a comfortable home with no mortgage, in a nice neighborhood, own an expensive vehicle, and be able to have enough money to do the things that I always wanted to do. To realize these dreams though, I knew I had to have a formula that generated a profit within the business. As George Melville, who with Jim Treliving built the Boston Pizza empire, once told a business group I was involved with, 'business isn't any fun if you don't make any money at it.'

I can still remember a number of years ago when my business had eight employees and generated approximately two million dollars in sales a year. I firmly believed we could be a $50 million company. This wasn't going to be achieved by mere luck. The company had many product ideas that we were attempting to get into the marketplace. Problem was, I did not have all of the proper equipment or resources to accomplish this.

I realized that to reach my dreams, I needed help—help from people who had better qualifications than me and knew more about certain areas of the business which I knew I would struggle at—especially if I was going to grow our business into the vision I had for it. To help move this process along, I knew the talent that I was hiring had dreams themselves. So, I tapped into asking them what their dreams were and told them what the company's goals and vision were. These goals and vision were of course, my dreams. Offering them the opportunity to reach their dreams allowed me to get "buy in" from them to move the company forward.

I remember dreaming that the company would be a large, progressive manufacturing facility offering products and services that not only met our customer's high expectations, but also mine. I wanted my company to be one that others looked at and viewed as a leader in their marketplace. To do this, I read about and observed other companies' success stories and copied their best practices and brought them to our company. I dreamt that if we could be the type of company that our clients wanted to do business with, success would follow."

Looking to the future, Dann naturally daydreams a bit differently than in elementary school—and to greater credit as well. Moving forward, he dreams to grow the business through acquisitions and create a more global company.

Are you like Dann in the way that matters most? Does your mind wander? During a class or meeting, do you find yourself staring out the window and daydreaming about what you'll do tomorrow or next week? As a child, were you constantly reminded by teachers to stop daydreaming?

If so, then welcome to the Daydreamers Club. Dann is by no means the sole member, but, as per Ampco's continued success, membership most clearly has it benefits. While most of us opt for a day pass, Dann shows us that with the Courage to Dream consistently, all things are possible.

Psychological research is beginning to reveal what Dann already knows—daydreaming is an indicator of an active and healthy brain. Despite what Dann's teachers may have told him, daydreaming is also a strong indicator of success. Researchers from the University of Wisconsin have discovered that daydreaming is linked to higher degrees of what is referred to as working memory. Cognitive scientists tell us that those with more working memory are defined by their ability to both focus and drift, making ample use the brain's ability to retain and recall information in the face of distraction.

The researchers conducting the study examined the relationship between people's working memory capacity and their tendency to daydream. They found a strong correlation between daydreaming and high scores on the working memory test. Why might this be the case? Could it be that the minds of daydreamers wander simply because the task at hand is often insufficient to require their full mental capacity—to say nothing of their apparent attention?

The researchers highlighted the likelihood that those with higher working memory capacities—and thus those who are naturally most prone to daydreaming—still have the ability to train themselves to focus their attention on what's in front of them—when necessary.

Mind wandering isn't free—it takes resources. But you get to decide how you want to use your resources. If your priority is to keep your attention on task, you can use working memory to do that, too.

We see this in Dann all of the time: daydreaming and highly-focused at the same time. It is who Dann is as a person that makes him a true leader.

Neuroscience has now shown that our brains do their best work when they wander: when we daydream. It's not when we are "trying to be creative" that any of us is at our best, but when we let go and dream along looser lines. That's when a still mysterious process in the right hemisphere of the brain, right behind the right ear makes connections between seemingly unrelated things, and those connections then bubble up as sudden insights, as if out of nowhere.

It is both an everyday daydreamer's delight, and as embodied by Dann, a powerful business tool—albeit one we too often keep tucked tightly in our heads.

Dann is fond of Einstein's quote on creativity and so are we. *"Creativity is the residue of time wasted."* Isn't that so true? Often the solutions to the most pressing issues come when we are not pressed to the desk, but out walking or relaxing.

Daydreaming gives Dann what it offers us all—insight. And while everyone has a dream, to gain that individual insight into any sized picture, we need to look within. There is a reason that they call it insight.

Neuroscience tells us what Dann has known all his life—there is a great power in the dreaming mind, especially in one wide awake. With the Courage to Dream, Dann makes far-reaching connections between seemingly unrelated ideas daily.

We can all do this. When we've really hit the wall, that's when we need to relax, stop thinking about work and wait a while. Answers arrive when we least expect them in the Daydreamers Club.

The next time someone catches you daydreaming on the job and asks you why you're not working, tell them you most certainly are hard at work. Our hope is that it works for you the way that it has worked for Dann Konkin and others.

Dann Konkin is a model of Courage.

22
Conclusion

Whether or not we are prepared to admit it, too many people are scared of life and full of fear. The good news as you now already know it doesn't have to be like that. Courage is a choice.

Unfortunately, there are still too many people living in the shadow of false though fatal fears and very real bullies alike. As a result, too many of us choose to live life under the harsh authority of someone else telling us what to think, what to view and what to do.

The reality of life is that the vast majority of people consistently choose fear over courage in all aspects of their lives. As a society we are dually-addicted to comfort and convenience.

The path in these pages is a bit more complex. The results are beyond belief.

We encourage you to walk the 10 Steps to Courageous Living and stride into a whole new way of being. You have our personal guarantee that your life will never be the same again.

Thank you for your time and courage . . . Ross & Bob

Ross Buchanan

As a Consultant to CEOs Ross works in a cross section of specialties including Business Development, Leadership, Recruiting, Strategic Planning, Crisis Management, Negotiating and as a Courage Coach. The author of four books, both fiction and non-fiction, Ross is a popular keynote speaker and workshop leader on the critical issue of Courageous Living in business and in life.

Ross is the creator of the Buchanan Courage Index (BCI) which is considered by many as one of the most effective systems of predicting sales and leadership success in North America today.

Professionally Ross is the Founder of Strategic Results International, a Leadership Development Firm and the CEO of Hunter Buchanan, a Sales and Leadership Recruiting Firm. Personally, Ross and his wife Charleen live in White Rock BC.

Bob Anderson

With an MBA from Royal Roads University and over twenty years of leadership experience Bob Anderson is someone who consistently inspires Courage in others. Bob's professional experience includes Sales, Marketing, Business Development and Strategic Planning. Bob is also an accomplished film maker and documentarian with such titles as "Leonard Peikoff In His Own Words" and "Ayn Rand In Her Own Words." Bob and his wife Denise live in Victoria BC.